BREAKING
THE BOX

I0475411

THE MOTIVATED MANAGER'S GUIDE
TO
ONLY-EXACTLY
RAPID PROCESS IMPROVEMENT

HOW TO IMPROVE PROFITS IN LESS THAN A WEEK

(WITHOUT SPENDING ANY MONEY)

PAUL E LEWIS

DEDICATION PAGE

This work is dedicated to all those who have challenged me, mentored me, tolerated me, listened to me, supported me, and allowed me to try new ideas in the workplace. For those who did none of these, I thank you too; for you provided me extra motivation to be a better employee, co-worker, and manager.

I'd also like to thank Denise for her expertise and support with this book. It would not exist without her effort.

And most importantly,

To Mary and Courtney—Thank You.

Contents

WHY READ ANOTHER BOOK?

Many years ago, I was 'invited' to join my colleagues in reading a book distributed to all the management team. The book was "The Goal" by Eliyahu Goldratt. This book was the first of many more books and hours of research striving to master Continuous Improvement.

The goal of "Breaking the Box" is to take one of the rapid process improvement tools I have used as a manager—Only-Exactly—and enable you as a motivated manager or business owner to put this useful process improvement principle into continuous use in your daily work life. This one tool has served me well, and I strive to teach it everyone that lets me do so.

As a business manager or owner, you know that time is one of, if not the most, precious resources required to run your business. Your time, your employee's time (which you pay handsomely for) and the company's time (which your customers pay you for). You know how much your employee's time is worth, but do you know how much YOUR time is worth. In order to make quality decisions for and about your business, it is imperative you attach a $$ value to YOUR time.

As a motivated manager, your goal is to run the most efficient, most productive, most respected operation possible. You realize that "status quo" and "barely making it" are for those who do not know how to or are lacking the drive to be the best. You may do it for the recognition. You may do it for the promotional opportunities. Or you may do it just for the satisfaction of being the best in your industry. Whatever your reasons, you are the motivated manager that will use this tool to excel.

You may have already used or be familiar with continuous improvement. While Only-Exactly, the tool we will be focusing on in this book, is only one tool used by continuous improvement experts, it is one that takes the least amount of time and produces the quickest, longest-lasting results. I am hoping to bring a deeper knowledge, understanding, and a new perspective to the improvements your gut tells you are correct even when you aren't sure exactly why they are.

If Only-Exactly is new to you, you will get an incredible bang for your buck. Opportunities to improve the workplace will start appearing to you that were there all the time, yet no one saw them. Not only will the changes save money, they will also foster a more cooperative work environment where management and employees don't have to be antagonistic when the business experiences change.

At the same time, if you are an experienced continuous improvement manager, you will also be able to pull off some very impressive improvements in your operation within a very short time. Why is this? The Only-Exactly technique is designed to use only the materials and resources you currently have available. In other words, your biggest expense should be the cost of celebrating your eventual achievements.

Whether you are a business manager or owner, or an employee with a goal to move into management, this book will place you in the unique position of being able to bring about improvements sooner. My hope is that you will be able to show at least a 10% to 20% improvement in the efficiency, quality, and/or productivity of your first targeted process.

If your first attempt does not meet this goal, do not give up or get discouraged. Facilitating improvement in your operation takes persistence, patience, and practice.

There will be tough decisions to make. Decisions will have to be measured and weighed against long-term goals, and. In fact, all improvements should be made with a long-term plan in mind.

There are obstacles that you will encounter as a motivated manager. You may feel resistance from all directions, but even a very small improvement in one solitary process can lead to a greater understanding of how to improve other departments or processes. I will share strategies for bringing not only your department online, but bringing the entire organization to a place where change is embraced rather than feared.

You will learn how to develop one of the strongest traits a motivated manager needs—persistence. But more than that, you will learn how to see the world from a new paradigm, one where you are successful as a manager and enable others to be successful operators within the system as well.

Becoming Box Clever

"Yesterday."

That was the answer given by the Director of Operations of the company that had just hired me to facilitate a turnaround of their worst performing facility. The question I had asked was, "What is your time expectation for me to bring this operation up to par?"

By any standard, fulfilling this expectation would be considered "Rapid." At the time, this particular facility rated consistently as the worst out of 14 facilities on almost every major benchmark. Every week, when the benchmarks were released for the previous week, and this facility was compared to the other facilities, it showed up with the bottom ranking.

It was a cold day in mid-January when I was given that goal. Eight weeks later, we broke into the top 3 on the weekly facility benchmarks. By the end of the year, we had finished in the top 3 spots on the weekly benchmarks 28 times in the last 42 weeks of the year. We finished as a Top 3 facility for that year, with the added distinction of improving from absolutely the worst facility in Service Quality, to #1 without equal.

How did this happen? It all began with a new paradigm. It began with recognizing that in business, finding multiple potential solutions for the issues that present themselves daily is preferable to accepting the first, or only) idea that the team can propose. The first need then is to develop the ability to see multiple potential solutions.

Let's look at the primary basic premise behind Only-Exactly—Breaking the Box.

Boxing Clever

"Thinking outside the box."

We hear this phrase in business conversations daily—so often it has almost lost its meaning. Every time I hear it, I wonder if the person using it knows what it really means to think outside the box.

The key to this wieldy concept is knowing HOW to do so.

In the classic puzzle that spawned this now trite phrase, the most famous 'solution' is often shown before the audience has an opportunity to solve it. Given the proper information and tools, those presented with the problem would have been able to take this problem apart and present MULTIPLE acceptable solutions that, in turn, could have then been evaluated for best fit for their situation.

If you are like so many business owners and managers today, you are probably inside the box struggling with how to think outside of it. You feel besieged by business goals, budgets, and projections. As you know from countless meetings, commercials, business books (like this one), and everyday conversations, inside the "Box" is where you are not suppose to be in your thinking.

Have you ever heard a definition of what the box is? Do you know what is it and why you are inside of it right now?

It's time to break the spell this 'box' has on everyone, smash this intangible concept into little pieces, and pile the pieces in the trash.

WHERE DID THIS BOX COME FROM?

The cliché comes from a puzzle consisting of nine dots in a 3x3 pattern drawn on paper. The goal is to draw as few straight lines as possible while passing through every dot without the writing utensil leaving the paper.

Upon first play, it seems difficult or impossible to do this with less than five straight lines. After some time the person who introduced the puzzle will show you how to accomplish this feat in FOUR lines by drawing the lines in a pattern that extends outside the visual box pattern that the nine dots create as shown in fig. 1 below.

In order to break the box, you must know what the box is. It is not really just a puzzle or drawing. "The box" is made up of an amalgamation of assumptions, experiences, and preconceived boundaries YOU, the problem solver bring with you when you are tasked with a problem to solve. Let's face it. It is very difficult to not bring your experience and knowledge to a problem, as these are the tools you have always used successfully before to solve problems.

When presented with the box puzzle, most people will mentally draw the walls of the box before they attempt to solve the puzzle. Those that introduce the "solution" often fail to provide all the other solutions to this puzzle. Some have taken on this puzzle and found that there are MANY solutions that are better while still meeting the conditions for solving the puzzle. There are so many more acceptable solutions that, if this were a competition, the 4-lines solution might not make it into the top ten.

If this were a manufacturing issue, the company that relied on the 4-line solution to give them a competitive advantage would be out of business in a short time. In order to gain a competitive advantage, a manager must first find out what the puzzle REALLY is asking and bring NO preconceived notions to cloud all the possibilities.

PICTURE THIS

Let's assume this nine-dot puzzle is a practical manufacturing/business process that, when improved or solved, will provide a competitive advantage. Your largest competitor, Less Lines Inc. has just brought to market the four straight lines solution. You are still operating with the five-line solution. You know that the "lines" process is 50% of the manufacturing cost of this product. Your competitor's four lines solution now gives them a 10% cost advantage and they are able to gain a significant competitive advantage in regards to price. In order to stay competitive, you must also bring to market a four-line or better solution.

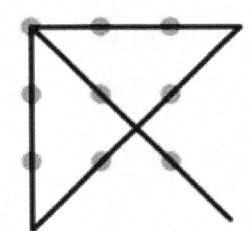

Fig. 1 - Four-line Solution

As soon as you learn of this, you call your R&D department manager and tell him you'll be right over. Soon you discover that Less Lines Inc. (LL I) has been "thinking outside the box". Being the competitive businessperson that you are, you head back to R&D determined to "break the box". By the end of the week you have a breakthrough. You discover how to solve the puzzle with three straight lines.

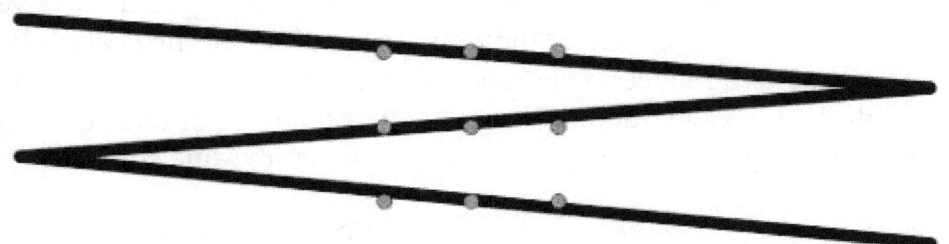

Fig. 2 - Three-line Solution #1

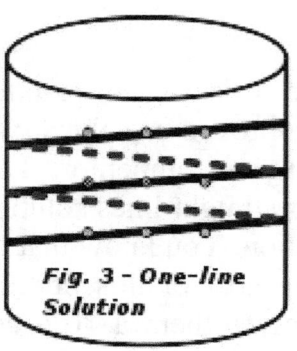

Fig. 3 - One-line Solution

This breakthrough leads to further discovery and you soon are capable of meeting the conditions of the process with only ONE straight line. Has your solution really "broken the box?" Or is there still waste in the process?

How Did You Reach Your One-Line Solution?

Once you realized that there were imaginary boundaries defined by the nine dots, you found you were able to remove all boundaries and assumptions, imaginary or not. First you defined the conditions of the process. In this case:

> First condition: fewest straight lines.
> Second: lines touching all dots.
> Third: writing utensil.
> Fourth: writing utensil cannot leave paper until finished.

After defining the conditions, you realized that all along you had introduced assumptions and boundaries upon the process. Since lines and dots have width, you realized the lines did not necessarily have to pass through the center of the dots. By angling the lines slightly, you were able to reduce the number of straight lines the dots passing through the lines to a total of three. The basic design of that solution was in the shape of a zigzag. You were on to a three-line solution.

After this success, you decided to take it further. If the dots were on a cylinder, you'd be able to observe all the rules. So you reached a viable one-line solution. You could stop there, but the goal of Only-Exactly is to never settle on one solution as the only solution.

MORE THAN ONE SOLUTION?

Take a closer look at the rules. The original puzzle said to use four lines? Is that necessary? You've already proven it isn't. Maybe some of the other "rules" should be looked at again.

> First condition: Use the fewest straight lines possible.
> Second: Pass through all dots.
> Third: Use a writing utensil that can draw a line.
> Fourth: Don't let the writing utensil leave the paper until finished passing through all the dots.

Look at the third condition "writing utensil". What is the definition of a writing utensil? It could be a pencil, a pen, a marker. The definition of a writing utensil is very loose.

Could your definitions be limiting you? If any system of marking paper could be considered a writing utensil, your options just expanded. There are marking tools that pass through all the dots simultaneously! You grab a fat marker and get the job done in one swipe.

But you don't stop there. As a motivated manager, you go on to discover many more solutions. Now you realize that you not only have a competitive advantage in the market for pricing, you should be able to lock in that competitive advantage with patents.

WHAT HAPPENED HERE?

Not a single rule was broken. What happened is this. ALL the unnecessary obstacles were removed. That's where you start. Drop what you or anyone else brings to the puzzle (like mentally connecting the dots) and deal ONLY with what is absolutely needed to accomplish the goal.

Some of the questions you could have asked yourself to get to this point include:

- ☐ How big are the dots?
- ☐ What is their diameter? All dots have a diameter. Only dots in mathematical theory have no diameter.
- ☐ How does this knowledge change the puzzle? With this knowledge, solving the puzzle with three lines as shown in Figure 2 is easy. Remember, the rules don't say that the lines must pass through the center of the dots.

What does that have to do with real-world applications? Consider this. If the dots have a dimension such as a diameter, then the lines used to solve the puzzle would also. How does that change the puzzle? Just because the puzzle is introduced on a two-dimensional plane doesn't mean conditions indicate that the solution must remain in two dimensions. Doesn't that open up a plethora of solutions?

At this point, you may have already realized that some of the more or 'less common' solutions (like the answer shown in Figure 3) aren't your only option. Personally, my favorite can be done with ONE line using the 'marking tool' most common to the Public Works department—a paintbrush.

Sure there are times when you have to stay inside the lines—like when you are driving down the road. Have you ever noticed that those 'Lines' are often many inches across. This line would easily pass all the conditions above.

For the nine-dot problem, there are a plethora of solutions that meet the conditions of the puzzle and are less than four lines. A quick Google search will yield websites that have pages dedicated to the many solutions found.

This box is broken. The best solutions for all problems come from not just thinking outside of the box but completely dismantling the box to determine ONLY EXACTLY what conditions are presented. In business, the same applies. Remove all assumptions and perceptions about the solution and the problem. Break down the problem to its most root definitions of the issue and define EXACTLY and ONLY what needs to happen.

One way to break it down is to realize that the only rules you can't break are the law and company policy. Other considerations would be ethics and culture; these are more intangible but are just as important when contemplating change.

If you get a feeling that you should bypass an excellent solution to the puzzle or problem because this solution doesn't seem to be in the spirit of solving problems the 'right' way, please banish this notion as soon as possible. The problem is the problem. The goal is to eradicate it. Do not protect the 'box'. Break your habit of doing this, and you will break the 'box' instead of being trapped into just thinking outside of it!

SO MANY BOXES

Opportunities to break boxes abound in every workplace, including yours right now. As any business grows, every department and process within that department or business needs to adjust to the changes and challenges growth brings. As a rule of thumb, every 20% change in volume for a department, business, or process is reason enough to reevaluate for improvements. As you grow to intimately know your business, department, and processes, you'll become more aware of how any and all changes in the business affect each process.

Only-Exactly Continuous Improvement

Over the past half-century, many different tools have been sold to businesses with the promise that this new methodology or continuous improvement tool will be the answer to all your operational issues. The truth is most of them can demonstrate a positive expectation when applied against most the issues you wish to resolve. The results for some of the problems you wish to solve may be adequate for the cost of training and implementation, however, it is unlikely that there is any one tool that is as simple to use as Only-Exactly. It is one of the best tools for solving the smaller operational issues that eat at a business daily.

A car mechanic typically spends many years building his toolbox with all kinds of tools and he makes sure he is able to use each one of them effectively. You should be building a toolbox of methodologies for Continuous Improvement and practicing daily to use them effectively for rapid process improvement. They are useful tools, but their focus is usually on a larger scale.

With Only-Exactly, we are going to extract some of the best tools from other improvement process methods. Only-Exactly scales these tools down so they are practical. Let's look at the most common continuous process improvement models. Like all methods for improving productivity, Only-Exactly is designed to make your operation or business leaner or less burdened with waste. It's just designed to do it a lot faster.

You may already know of all or most of the methods that follow, or you may have heard of only a few. Each one contributes to the concept behind Only-Exactly.

I will keep the definitions and explanations simple. You may find much more in-depth information about these on the Internet.

LEAN MANUFACTURING (MUDA)

Lean is the basic concept of waste reduction through process improvement and has become a generic term and management philosophy for waste reduction efforts.

The idea of Lean is to target all waste within a system or process and eliminate it. It focuses on optimizing flow and using different methods (like some of the ones mentioned below) to determine the value of every resource in a business system as it relates to the customers' expectations and needs.

Toyota is generally recognized as the first company to develop Lean. It is recognized as one of the first and most successful Continuous Improvement programs ever developed, and still seen in action today in the Toyota Production System (TPS). A Japanese term you may also hear related to Lean is "Muda" which means an activity that is wasteful and does not add value.

In order to help identify waste, Lean breaks out seven specific things to look for that are, by nature, waste within a process or system. An acronym has been created for these seven types of waste— TIMWOOD.

T: Transportation; *i.e. unnecessary movement of product*
I: Inventory; *i.e. raw materials, work-in-progress (WIP), or finished goods which tie up capital, space, and also allow for shrink (damaged goods)*
M: Motion; *i.e. unnecessary motion of the workers and/or equipment*
W: Waiting; *i.e. any goods or products waiting for the next step in the process*
O: Over-processing; *i.e. producing more goods than demand calls for*
O: Over-production; *i.e. more work than is necessary for a product to meets customer's needs or expectations*
D: Defect; *i.e. extra costs associated with correcting any defects in material or goods*

Reduction of any or all of these in a business or manufacturing system is the ongoing goal of Lean. Most of the gains from the Only-Exactly method will be seen in the Motion, Transportation, and Waiting areas.

For example, anytime you reduce the motions of your operators, you almost always see improvements in labor efficiency. If you eliminate unnecessary movement of product, you reduce total labor hours. And if you can eliminate bottlenecks of goods or products waiting to move on to the next process, you improve the total output capacity of the organization.

A well-known example of reducing operator motion with no reduction in product motion is a Bucket Brigade. In a bucket brigade, a line of people pass a bucket or other item from person to person. The bucket moves along with little motion from each individual. If each person were to carry each bucket individually, he or she would tire quickly. The line would slow down, eventually requiring the people to stop and rest much sooner.

The methods and tools presented in this book can be considered a Lean method, however when I talk about Only-Exactly, I'm not focusing on 'removing' or 'reducing' waste from processes or systems. Instead, Only-Exactly focuses on rebuilding the process by starting with ZERO waste and adding ONLY what is necessary. Rebuilding the process enables you to consider every resource, function, movement, and event as it contributes to the expectations and needs of the subsequent processes in the system and ultimately the end user or customer. More on that later.

SIX SIGMA

Six Sigma is a continuous improvement process that serves to improve quality or results of a business through a very guided set of steps. The facilitators of these projects are specially trained in the process of Six Sigma and are most commonly known as Master

Black Belts, Black Belts, and Green Belts. The level of facilitator assigned depends on the scope and size of the project.

Six Sigma is very heavy in statistical data and was designed using many different forms of business improvement methodologies and concepts. This method has received criticism for not being original and drawing from many already established continuous improvement methodologies and for not accounting for the actual quality demands of the specific business.

The real issue isn't lack of originality. Six Sigma just isn't a good fit for many businesses. It can be very effective for large-scale improvement projects. Some businesses and products need stricter quality control and benefit from Six Sigma. Others suffer from the law of diminishing returns when this methodology is applied to their industry, possibly losing competitive advantage due to the increased costs imposed by unnecessary quality levels. In addition, it can be a very time-consuming and labor-intensive program, a problem made even worse if a project is compromised by bad data.

The main purpose of Six Sigma is to improve the Quality of the process and end product, which by nature is a form of reducing waste. It is often paired with Lean concepts and called Lean Six Sigma in order to add some focus on waste reduction during the Six Sigma process.

The Six Sigma methods typically use one of two sets of methodology, DMAIC and DMADV. Both methods are effective and are very similar in implementation.

D: Define the problem.	D: Define the problem.
M: Measure the process and collect data.	M: Measure the process and collect data.
A: Analyze the data.	A: Analyze the data.
I: Improve the process.	D: Design and optimize the process.
C: Control the process.	V: Verify the design and implement.

KAIZEN

Kaizen is Japanese for "improvement" or "change for the better". Kaizen is basically a philosophy and set of practices focused on continuous improvement of processes in manufacturing and business. It focuses more on the humanization of the processes and workplace and involves the participation of as many people as possible in the improvement process. Kaizen becomes part of the culture of a business when at its best.

A Kaizen Event (or Blitz) is a short-term rapid process improvement project similar to Only-Exactly but focuses on mapping the process and reducing or removing waste. A Kaizen Event can be very effective for short-term improvements and to promote a cooperative culture in a workplace environment.

Kaizen is most like Only-Exactly in its structure. Kaizen focuses on the operators, the mapping of the process, and the reduction of the waste in the process. It usually targets a larger system of processes but is effective at most levels. Kaizen and Only-Exactly both work best when they are part of the culture of the workplace including every operator as a part of the improvement process.

The biggest difference is the directions in which both attack the problem of waste. Only-Exactly starts with one thing and rebuilds the process with as little waste as possible and Kaizen starts with the whole process and works to remove waste from the process. It is my belief that rebuilding with as little waste as possible makes getting to the goal—completely eliminating waste—faster and more efficient.

THEORY OF CONSTRAINTS (TOC)

Theory of Constraints, also known as Constraints Management, is a methodology used to identify system constraints and restructure the organization or department around improvement of the constraint or bottleneck in the system. This concept was first introduced by Eliyahu Goldratt in his book *The Goal.* It is a book I recommend for anyone interested in continuous improvement.

The Theory of Constraints is based on the idea that every system is constrained by one process within that system. The constraint determines the absolute throughput of the system. By controlling the constraint process, one is able to control the system throughput and the ultimately the rest of the system.

The five steps used to improve and control the system are:

1. Identify the constraint.
2. Decide how to exploit the constraint.
3. Subordinate all other processes to the above decision.
4. Elevate the constraint.
5. If the constraint has moved to another process, return to Step #1. Do not let inertia be the constraint.

TOC works very well with Only-Exactly. When picking your first target process, it helps to have an understanding of the constraints of the business and operations. Focusing on the constraint as your first targeted process can provide improvement to the entire business and operation. Only-Exactly is one way to exploit and elevate the constraint. Then you can work on the processes closely tied with the constraint provide even more opportunity.

KANBAN

The impact of the Japanese on continuous process improvement shows up in this word as well. Kanban loosely means "card signal" or "visible symbol". A Kanban is a sign or signal meant to trigger an action within a process to increase efficiency or timeliness of a supported task in a process.

An example of a Kanban may be a plastic card, an empty cart, a small flag, or empty floor space that signals for an operator to initiate a task such as replenishment or material movement. Kanban typically focuses on operators or those who handle replenishment of material. The Kanban helps with Just-in-Time (JIT) functions to ensure that materials or supplies are available when and where needed.

Kanban is also a part of Toyota's Lean methodology to reduce wasted time waiting for materials and to reduce overproduction from a preceding process in the system. It operates from the perspective of 'pulling' product through the system rather than 'pushing'.

POKA-YOKE (ERROR-PROOFING)

A poka-yoke is a change, a modification, mechanism, or tool in a process to eliminate defects. It is a designed failsafe to completely eliminate the potential for a defect within the product or process, or at least alert an operator of defects occurring in a process.

You will find examples of poka-yoke in everyday life. The inability in late model cars to change gears from Park to Drive without first applying the brake is one such example. An electrical plug having one prong wider than the other so that it cannot be plugged into an outlet backwards is an example that has been around for quite a few years.

A well-designed poka-yoke is capable of completely eliminating specific defects or potential issues in a process or product. A well-implemented poka-yoke is capable of completely eliminating specific defects in a process. Typically, they are most effective at the operator/equipment level.

5S

The 5S's are based on five Japanese words that represent steps in what can be best described as process improvement through housekeeping. One English translation of the 5S words is Sort, Set in Order, Shine, Standardize, Sustain.

The method typically involves everyone in the department or target area. The idea is to completely remove all items, equipment, or materials not necessary for the processes in that immediate area. Those items that are not used frequently are placed where they are out of the way until needed but not so far away that it slows production when that item is needed. All tools, equipment, and material have a designated spot to be stored when not in use. Cleanliness and clear visual cues for the movement within the department are a focus.

In my experience, Only-Exactly is more efficient. During one 5S project, we targeted a simple issue—replacing 55-gal. barrels of adhesive/sealant on a barrel pump when one ran dry. Barrel replacement was the process immediately preceding the constraint in the department meaning every minute that the pump was not running while the barrels were being replaced, production was at a dead stop.

We found that the operators were spending at least 5 minutes looking for the tools and wrenches needed to replace the barrels. Over time, wrenches would disappear until there was one set for the three pumps that were about 100 ft from each other. The operators would travel from pump to pump until they found a full set of tools to replace the barrel. This happened at least 5 times per day on a 24-

hour workday. About 30 minutes per day the entire operation was not producing while the operators were searching for tools.

The fix was simple. We purchased enough tools to make 3 full sets (one for each pump) and tethered the tools to the pump frame with cable wire. For less than $100, the department increased productivity by 2% almost instantly. The improvement paid for itself with ONE barrel change.

The whole 5S project took a couple of months to complete. If we had simply targeted that one process with Only-Exactly, the problem would have been identified within in minutes, resolved with one trip to the hardware store and paid for itself in just a couple of hours.

JUST-IN-TIME (JIT)

JIT is often used synonymously with the Toyota Production System. The concept is to focus on flow through the system by providing the necessary materials and resources only when they are needed. JIT helps focus attention on the handling of materials and work-in-progress in order to reduce the wastes of over-production, inventory, and waiting. The main objective is for all required materials to arrive at the process only when they are needed by that process. Kanban is an essential function in JIT.

JIT primarily focuses on reducing the wastes associated with over-production, waiting, over-processing, and inventory. In a perfect JIT production system, there is no waiting at all. All resources arrive at the precise moment needed and would not stop when moving from one process to another.

If all processes take exactly the same amount of time then there will be no waiting, however, this is next to impossible to achieve in a real operation. Many factors influence processing time including maintenance, repairs, quality issues, and/or force majeure. The downside comes because the time spent in one process usually takes

longer than another. Trying to achieve balance then become a major challenge.

VALUE STREAM MANAGEMENT

The value stream is a full cycle business process mapping method used to understand the business system and more importantly which processes within the system add value to the product or service. The processes in a value stream are typically categorized three ways: value added, non-value added, and non-value added but necessary.

'Value-added' are those processes in the value stream that the customer or consumer is willing to pay for in the offered product or service. 'Non-value-added' are the processes or functions that add no value. These would be the focus for elimination since they are waste. 'Non-value-added but necessary' are those functions that add no value but are necessary to ensure the business or operation remains in compliance with policy, safety, and/or laws.

VISUAL FACTORY

Visual factory is a means of communicating with the operators and other employees in order to provide information on the processes and productivity of an operation or business. It is basically a way to communicate to and amongst operators information on how they as a group or department are doing with productivity.

The visual factory method also acts as a motivator when operators see how their efforts contribute to the success of the business. Visual Factory can also be combined with goal-setting to inform everyone of progress towards a common or department goal. Digital counters, productivity billboards, and even real-time television feeds are some of the tools used in Visual Factory.

Your Tool Chest

Only-Exactly can be seen as one tool amongst many. Or it can be seen as a tool that takes the best features of some very useful tools and makes it possible to apply the principles of continuous improvement rapidly.

Many times a business will adopt a new methodology like Six Sigma and expect that it will be the ultimate program to end waste or improve operations. Soon they discover that it works well for a while, but then seems to fade. This is due, in part, to the expectation that one method is best for all business problems or is the best tool for improving every process in their business.

You can use an adjustable plumber's wrench to loosen most any bolt, but it's not as efficient as using a wrench that's the exact fit for the bolt. A hammer is great for nails, but does not work well with screws or staples typically. You need a variety of tools in the tool chest. Each process has an Improvement Methodology that works better than other methods for improving the process you want to target. You want to have a working knowledge of as many methods as possible in order to pick the best one for the process you are going to target for improvement.

You may have noticed that many of the methods above overlap and have concepts in common. For instance, Kanban, Visual Factory, and 5S all use forms of visual cues to communicate to the operators. Value Stream Management and Kaizen Events use process mapping to evaluate their processes and systems. These tend not to be particularly rapid improvements but are very effective.

Only-Exactly with its method of 'breaking the box' is a strong tool you can add to your ever-growing toolbox of continuous improvement knowledge. Its focus is on rapid change, at minimal cost, adds a dimension to continuous improvement that most businesses don't realize they can use.

As a motivated manager, you can turn you or your employer's business into a more profitable operation with this one tool, even if you cannot implement any of the other process management tools we've covered in this chapter.

Rapid Results – How Rapid is Rapid?

In terms of process improvement, how rapid is rapid? In the case of the 9-dot puzzle, we were working to bring solutions to the table in a matter of minutes. In the real world with real operations, things don't move quite that quickly. In most businesses today, standard process improvement projects can take as little as four weeks and as many as two years depending on the scope and goal of the project.

With Only-Exactly, our expectation for rapid could be as little as a few hours before improvement is observed or it may be a couple of weeks. In order to be considered rapid, the initial discovery and initiation of the improvement should be approximately two weeks. One week to research and plan, and one week to make the changes and tweak for best results, if needed.

The purpose of this method to bring you results in as soon as one-day and no longer than two weeks.

After two weeks, you should start to see the improvements solidifying within the system. The changes made should naturally be improving as a part of the system and the surrounding processes.

The scope and scale that we will be working with will range from as small as one discrete process and may scale up to a manufacturing production line or department. In this case, "rapid" will be defined as two weeks down to as little as one hour.

You will find that the bigger the project's scope, the longer it takes exponentially to experience results due to the involvement and input needed from more people and/or departments. It takes some practice to gauge how much input you need from other departments on a larger project. That's why starting with small Only-Exactly projects is so important.

Your first rapid process improvements should focus on a single or simpler process within your department. Look for a project that will take no longer than two days. Avoid making changes or focusing on improvements that are immediately preceded or followed by another department. Instead, focus your initial improvements in the 'middle' of your department in order to observe the results and affects of your changes to see if there are any unexpected results. In addition, you will have more control over the changes and the results.

Do not get discouraged if the first improvements show little to no results right away. Here is what typically happens. Immediately after a change, those operators directly affected need some time to learn the new system/processes or need time to internalize the alteration in their routine. The amount of time the operator needs to learn and master the changes depends on the extent the changes contrast with their old routine.

A rule of thumb is if the changes immediately show the same or slightly better performance in the process, the process improvement will show even stronger results when the operators master and embrace the new routine.

After a couple of 2-day improvements, look to take on something that takes a week or so and build up from there. As you build up, you may notice that some larger improvement projects will actually make changes to processes you have already worked on. This is normal.

Always make improvements that increase the overall productivity of your department, even if it requires altering something you thought worked well before. Know that it is very likely that eventually you will make changes to all of the processes in your department more than once, sometimes multiple times as your projects grow in scope. No process is sacred and no change is permanent.

You are not trying to hit home runs with each improvement. It's the many small improvements that multiply and grow results exponentially within your department. In the beginning, you are familiarizing yourself with the process of Only-Exactly rapid process improvement and slowly perfecting it. In effect, with each improvement you make within your department, you are making another small improvement to your management skillset.

Move up to 2 weeks eventually—one week to break it down and plan, and one week to implement and fine-tune. Implementation usually takes a few hours at most. After that it is very important to take the rest of the week to carefully observe the changes, get feedback from the operators, make sure the changes stick, and watch the results grow.

You may find that one obstacle of rapid process improvement is obtaining good information from other departments in your facility or company. The priorities of your department's projects and goals have little bearing on other department's priorities. When making changes that affect other departments or when needing specific information, expect delays and to get resistance. In cases like these, attempt to create a situation where the other department can also benefit from the cooperation. In some cases, the other department will see MORE benefit from your process improvements than you will see in your department.

Start small and work up to the whole department eventually. When the other managers see the progress you've made and the results, they may ask you to show them what you did to get that level of improvement. Help them out.

Helping the business do well is a team effort. Share what you are learning and strong partnerships between your department and others within the business may develop. Working together, you may be able to facilitate some of those improvements that you could never accomplish without the help of the other managers. I have seen whole facilities and regional centers impacted by Only-Exactly.

If you are tackling processes that span more than one department or directly or indirectly affect other processes in the operation, you may need to look at stepping up to one of the more involved techniques like lean six Sigma or 5S. These are very good methods and tools, but they tend to take multiple weeks or months and tend to be rather labor consuming as well.

We will be drawing upon the knowledge base of the "big project" tools like lean Six Sigma, 5S, TOC (Theory of Constraints), and Kaizen in order to support the changes we will make. But Only-Exactly downsizes these "big project" tools so that any motivated manager can identify quick and inexpensive improvements that improve the working environment.

If I were to use the Only-Exactly portion of the rapid process improvement method on this book, this chapter would probably be the only one and it would be rather short. However, the actual goal is to bring a full understanding of the method to you so that you can not only use it effectively; hopefully you will be able to teach it to others as well.

When approaching a target process or processes to improve, you want to understand that 'improvement' is a misnomer in this case. The goal is not to 'improve' the process but rather to re-build it. Over time and through changes, processes get weighed down with unnecessary waste. Sometimes the waste is built into the process from the beginning. Almost all of the methods used today approach processes when they are loaded with waste and try to 'pick out' the bad parts of the process, we are going to break the box by starting with Only-Exactly what the process is supposed to accomplish and add only what is necessary to meets the needs of the rest of the business.

Sometimes you will find that the result of breaking the box is a radical departure from the usual modus operandi within your company or industry. This is good; it generally means you will see significant results from the changes.

However, such radical change can and usually will be met with resistance from all sides. Once you have proven your adeptness at making noticeable and sustainable 'improvements', trust will increase and you will be able to tackle the radical changes that may even revolutionize the industry.

OPERATORS

Throughout the examples and explanations in this book, I have chosen to use the term "operators" to describe the individuals who are involved in the actual implementation of a process. I use this term in place of more common terms such as employee, worker, or team member. Use of this term also reduces confusion with the "team members" who participate on the improvement teams.

I have done this to highlight the significance of those who perform or "operate" the processes. Operators are integral to the success of any business as well as any improvements or changes to the processes of that business. They are more than just employees or workers. They are the "operators" within the processes and their behavior influences the success of every process change.

The operators are the most flexible and the most influential element of every process. You will find most of the improvements you hope to achieve will be closely tied with the motions, behaviors, and motivations of your operators. Respect their value and treat them well.

STEP ONE: PICK THE TARGET PROCESS

Picking your very first process to target will be explored more thoroughly in a later chapter since you will be on the verge of breaking your first box by that time and it is most important in terms of being successful. After you have completed a few rapid process improvements, the possibilities open up and you find that ANY process can be targeted. Every process and department can be and should be a target for improvement eventually. So, if you don't already know where the process with the most potential is, ask yourself these questions:

- What process uses the most resources?
- What process is performed more often than any other; hundreds, even thousands of times in one day?
- What process seems to slow up the whole department?
- Where is work stacking up?
- What process requires operators to travel the most?
- What process do I know the least about?

The two biggest targets are the processes that answer the first two questions above. Those processes typically have the most opportunity built into them for large productivity gains. If you do one process, one thousand times in one shift, reducing that process by one second will net you over 16 minutes of time saved. This is a lot of labor hours when multiplied over your department for a full year. Those 16 minutes are a 3.5% improvement for one operator alone. If you can shave just 5 seconds off that process, that's 80 minutes of labor saved or a 17.5% productivity improvement. Avoid improving process that take little time and are only done a couple times per day. Improving a process by one minute per cycle that is done two or three times per day, is only 2-3 minutes and it's much easier to improve a process by one second versus one minute.

Be careful when targeting processes that are limited by another process. You can usually still show some improvement but you may need to target the process that limits other processes first. This can be the constraint or bottleneck or one of the constraints in the department. You may see more improvement overall if you target one of those constraints first.

STEP TWO: BUILD YOUR TEAM

Once you have determined the process you will be targeting, you can now build the team you will need to accomplish the changes. Much like a Kaizen Event, you will want to bring together enough people with the pertinent knowledge of the process as well as those who are downstream to ensure the changes you make will not adversely affect their processes. At first, when you start small, the team might only consist of you, a lead or supervisor, and maybe the operator whose process you are targeting. Try to keep the team as small as possible but include those in the supervisory chain who will need to know and understand what will be changing. This also provides the opportunity for you to teach and mentor them. Hopefully, you soon will give them a chance to target a process within their domain.

If you want to practice a little before bringing together a team, pick a process or two that YOU do on a regular basis and run the steps on it. You may be able to complete this in a day or less depending on how often you normally do the process.

STEP THREE: ONLY-EXACTLY

The next step is to break the target process down to its Only-Exactly. This is where there will typically be some debate. What usually happens is that the team truly believes that every step of the target process, as it exists at that moment, is necessary and justifiable. This may be the hardest part for your team. It is up to you to help them understand that, for instance, walking over to pick up a wrench from the toolbox is NOT necessary, the use of the wrench may be necessary but the walking over to the toolbox is definitely not.

Start with exactly what the target process is supposed to accomplish, the simple goal of the process. Any motion, step, function, communication, paperwork, travel, movement, or thought presently in the target process that does not DIRECTLY affect the process in the completion of this goal is waste, period. Some of those steps are necessary for the function of the business but those will be selectively added to the process only as needed.

> *Brainstorming with no limits is a great way to get ideas on how to rebuild the process. No idea is too crazy since that insane idea may be the catalyst for a revolutionary epiphany.*

Be careful not to unintentionally add steps or unnecessary items to the Only-Exactly. For instance, if part of a process requires a tool to be used, do not add the step of 'picking up the tool'. Someone may argue that you HAVE to pick up the tool to use it, this may be true but it is not NECESSARY to do. So, you may want to describe this Only-Exactly as "tool removes excess weld" or "tool tightens bolt". Right? Wrong. In this case, we have made the error of also including the tool in the Only-Exactly. The tool may be the most practical way, or it actually may be the only way to "remove excess weld" or "tighten bolt", but it is NOT part of the Only-Exactly because the only important part of the process is simply removing the excess weld or tightening the bolt, nothing else. When you are able to see all those obstacles or assumptions that you unintentionally and automatically bring to the problem, only then will you be able to resolve issues or make improvements that truly 'break the box'.

If after you've found that using the tool in question is the most practical and most efficient way to accomplish the Only-Exactly, then you can move on to how to use the tool. To not 'pick up the tool', you can make the tool already be 'up' and in place to use. Build a hanging tether for the tool to be as close to where it is applied as possible. It may even be possible to mount the tool where it can automatically perform the function within the process without being touched by the worker. Consider these items only when you have completely broken down the process, until then this is really just waste.

In another example from everyday life, technology now allows us to function on an Only-Exactly basis with the modern Smartphone and Bluetooth. Thirty years ago, when we decided to call Mom (again), we would need to move to the telephone which was attached to the wall or sitting on a table due to the physical phone line need to connect to the phone company. We would pick up the receiver, put it to our ear, listen for a dial tone, and dial the number in the rotary dial (or punch the number into the buttons). Now we have the technology available to simply say, "Call Mom" and all of the functions we were used to doing are handled now on an almost instant basis. The Only-Exactly in this case is, 'call Mom', all you have to do is say it, which would be the only added function in this 'process'. The Only-Exactly is what has to happen, not what is done with tools, people, or resources to make it happen.

As a rule, the Only-Exactly in its most simple form will consist of only two words. The first word is typically an action/verb; the second an object/noun. Like the examples "tighten bolt" and "call Mom", the action is followed by the object of that action only. There are no specifics on "How". That is built into the process later by your team with available resources. In the other example, "remove excess weld", there is one adjective that is more specific to the process. Extra qualifiers for the Only-Exactly should be for quality standards or specifics for the operator to ensure the process meets the customer's expectations for quality.

In most cases, you will find that the process consists of only one or two actual steps that are absolutely necessary. The rest is waste that you must eliminate or minimize with available resources. When we get to the examples, you will be able to see just how little actually NEEDS to be accomplished in your department and company to meet your customers expectations, how much are support functions for those few important steps, and how much is simply waste.

You should have a list of ALL the ideas. If every possible idea has been noted, then you must have one that simply says, "change nothing". Often, that is the first one to be submitted and

typically should be the first one you dismiss. Go through each and every idea/proposal and set aside all those that require any resources that you would need to rebuild the process other than what you have available to you right now (or can get from another location for little cost).

STEP FOUR: REBUILD THE PROCESS

One of the goals of this book is to minimize the actual cost of process improvement as well as reduce the time it takes to implement. When rebuilding processes, always try to do so with ZERO dollar outlay. Use ALL the resources, equipment, labor, knowledge, and ingenuity available to you before spending one dollar of your budget. You could argue that labor is from your budget; it is, but it is a resource that is already available at your location. Be careful not to add labor unnecessarily to the process or to not account for a change that simply displaces the labor to another process or department. This may be an actual improvement for both processes; however, it may not be well received by other departments when you inadvertently change their processes without notice. Watch carefully where the labor goes, it can be misleading.

Now that you have the process broken down to its Only-Exactly, it is time to rebuild the process with as little waste as possible. Depending on the target process, you can either make a floor layout on a large piece of paper (like on a presentation easel) or on a dry-erase board. If the process is confined to a relatively small area, you may want to do this part at the actual location of the process in the facility.

Once you have the layout where everyone can picture what is happening, start by adding only what you absolutely have to add to the location to complete the task/process. Remember the concept of micro-logistics and minimize all movement within the process and location. Create the situation where the operator can do as much of the process without taking one step in any direction. Create the situation where the Only-Exactly happens in the shortest path possible through the area. Create a work area void of everything but only what is needed to meet the requirement of the process, the customer's expectations, business needs, and an environment for the worker to excel. At times, you will find that simply creating a work area for the worker to excel in speed and quality will bring significant gains in productivity and efficiency.

Rebuild the process with the fewest number of steps possible; even a simple step, like picking up a tool, adds time to the process. Explore different ways of doing the same thing. Think of crazy ideas, then hypothetically walk through the process using the crazy ideas. Do not stifle creativity, the more you explore the process the more you will learn about this process and be able to apply that knowledge at a later date when you are rebuilding another process.

For some, this is the most fun of all the steps. You can view it just like a puzzle; you have all the pieces; the Only-Exactly, the equipment, the operators, available labor, knowledge, crazy ideas, and an opportunity to make your department or company better. Put the pieces together using the least amount of tangible and available resources for the best result.

Do not forget to factor in events that externally affect the process like breaks and lunches, bottlenecks/constraints ahead of the process that limit resources like available work to that process, and quality standards that may place time limits on the process. If the constraint in the department is preceding the process you are targeting, you may not be able to improve the output of that process due to the limitations of input to the process. However, do not let that deter you from eventually targeting any process; you may still be able to show

improvement by being able to move some labor from that process to the constraint to increase flow.

Other factors that can be positively or negatively affected by improvement projects other than quality may be less tangible like workplace culture, ethical/fair treatment, company policy, and, most importantly, safety. Factor all those in when rebuilding any process, especially safety.

When you feel you have some solid scenarios and layouts in place, move out into the work area where the process takes place (if you are not already there) and walk through it with the team. See if you can spot potential issues and hammer them out right there if possible. Sometimes you will have to go back and move the pieces of the puzzle around some more. Remember you are not trying to hit a home run with your first attempt or with any attempts for that matter, you want to be able to see a 5-10% improvement soon after implementation. Often that initial 5-10% will grow as you watch the new improved process in action and fine-tune it. Ask for feedback, as the other operators may be able to see something you cannot or are not aware of. The more you listen and the more you watch the processes in action, the more you know all there is to know about how all the processes work together to accomplish (or struggle to accomplish) the goals of your department.

Know that all the improvements and changes you have made are really only temporary. As your business or company grows and changes, the demands on each process within the business and company change. What is the most efficient, most productive way to perform a process today will need to be rebuilt sometime in the future to handle the changes. If you are with the company long enough, there is a good chance you will be revisiting a process you once mastered months or years previous. However now you already have the experience with this process and knowledge of the layout and resources. You may even be able to make the improvements on the fly and see the results in minutes.

Presently over 90% of the cranberries harvested each year are collected by completely flooding the cranberry field, then knocking the fruit off the vine to allow the cranberries to float to the surface.

Water harvesting was first tried in the 1850's. Back then the idea was considered a failure. Not until the 1960's was water harvesting successful.

Someone in the 1850's was brave enough to suggest flooding the farm simply to harvest cranberries. Someone in the 1960's was brave enough to suggest flooding the farm again, a process that had previously been considered a failure. Today, it saves cranberry farmers a considerable amount of money in harvesting costs.

What made the difference? In the 1850s, freezing the fruit before processing was not available. So farmers had to make sure their berries weren't bruised, or they didn't ship well. Today, over 90% of the cranberry crop is processed into juice, frozen or canned within days of harvest. This accounts for the fact that less than 10% of the farmers growing cranberries still harvest by hand.

One day a department head approached me with a problem. They had received a request to work on a special project within the department. They felt they were currently understaffed to handle their present responsibilities, much less a special project which would require 8 to 12 hours additional per day. At the time the department had a staff of five operators, one lead, and the department head.

The first thing we did was determined how much actual labor was required to do Only-Exactly what was needed in that department. We sat down and listed every function where actual labor hours were needed over the course of a week. We found multiple redundancies within the daily tasks of that department. These were not obvious redundancies but became apparent when the functions and necessary tasks were broken down to Only-Exactly what was needed from that department.

To our surprise, the actual labor hours needed for that department worked out to 13 hours per day on average. This information facilitated quick completion of the special project, additional support for other departments dealing with the same project, and a significant increase in productivity and effectiveness for the entire facility.

Always be mindful that changes in one department can significantly affect upstream and downstream departments or processes. If you are not sure whether a specific process or change affects another part of the business, be sure to find out before setting those changes in motion.

Before you get to actually picking your first target, it will help to visualize the steps in action. It's time to give some examples of what it looks like to break the box in the real workplace.

Each of the following examples are based upon real events, however some of the specific details about processes and functions have been changed for security or confidentiality reasons. In each example, I expect to demonstrate that just about any process in business can be targeted and improved with these steps and this method.

PRODUCT HANDLING DEPARTMENT – DISTRIBUTION CENTER

The Little Department

This department was part of much larger operation in a distribution facility. It was unique in that it handled a special subset of product that had certain rules for ordering and shipping. Due to their value, each item on each order had to be documented and tracked separately in preparation for shipping it to the customer.

Step #1-Picking the Target Process

The process that was targeted in this department included all handling and packaging of the goods. On an average night, there were 6 operators needed to complete the orders, which usually ran about 1000 line items.

When the orders drifted above 1000 line items, overtime was just about guaranteed. On one shift when the line items reached 1300, not only was the department going to have to stay late, but it also risked missing the shipping deadline.

This level of volume pushed the shift well past ten hours for sure and, since this department's volume had been steadily increasing

over the last year, it was only going to get more difficult to meet the deadlines for that department. Something had to be done.

Step #2- Build the Team

Every person in the chain of command from the Manager to the Lead was invited to the Team. I explained that we were going to streamline the processes in this department—specifically the handling and packaging processes. As a primer during that first meeting, I presented them with their first problem to solve—the nine-dot puzzle. That is when they were introduced to the concept of 'Breaking the Box'.

Step #3-Only-Exactly

Since this was a multi-step process, there were a number of 'Only-Exactlies' to eventually consider. Now that the team had a grasp of what we were looking for, it was time to break it down.

We started by breaking the entire target process down to the most basic Only-Exactly. In order to help the team understand the concept better, I asked them what was the end result of that targeted process. The agreed upon answer was 'shipped orders'. I asked them if people doing the actual work were "shipping orders"?

They said, "No, they are picking and packaging the products."

"Excellent, so they are not 'shipping orders' they are picking and packaging products, correct?"

"Yes."

"So, what is the simple end result of this process?'

They mulled it over and agreed that it was 'packaged products'. "There you go," I said, "So what is the one simple thing that this process accomplishes?"

"Package products." That is it. All of the work that is done by the operators and all the time spent doing the work is to accomplish one thing—package products. That was the primary "Only-Exactly." Now that we knew the Only-Exactly, we could focus on rebuilding the process.

Along with any process, there are a number of compliance factors that need to be considered and accommodated. Right after you establish the main Only-Exactly is a good time to list all those sub-processes that must happen to be compliant with policy, safety, and law.

Be cautious when building this list as you can inadvertently add processes that are not necessary. If you are unsure, find out before you implement the changes if you can.

One of the goals of this method is to do the entire project for zero dollars, other than the labor directly involved with the project. 90% of all projects can be done spending exactly zero dollars and still easily achieve the goal of 5 to 10% in measurable improvement.

Any time you absolutely have to use capital, try to spend no more than $100. If you spend more than that on any project, you want to see significant gains. Unless you have gone through every process in your location and are revisiting processes that can be significantly improved with a small capital purchase, focus on Only-Exactly projects that don't cost anything.

Step #4- Rebuilding the Process

We went out to the location in the department where the packaging process occurred and began by hypothetically performing the Only-Exactly. (Note: If your floor location is in use, you can run through the steps on a dry erase board or on a large sheet of blank paper.)

- We took one item and put it in packaging. The steps to package one item would be the basic steps to accomplish the goal of the process.
- We looked at how to minimize the movement of the operators to accomplish these steps and still have room to meet all of our compliance requirements and still have enough work-in-progress to keep the process flowing as smoothly as possible.
- We walked through multiple scenarios to see what series of events/steps minimized the movement of the items, operators, and packaging that also provided room in the process for all compliance related steps.

I also asked the team a number of questions to get them thinking about making the process very efficient with the least amount of waste possible.

- Can we move the packaging closer to the product?
- Can we move the product closer to the packaging?
- Can we minimize the movement of the operator moving the product?
- Can we minimize the actual movement of the product?
- Are the operators picking up the same product more than once?
- Can we batch similar orders together in small batches to minimize movement of those moving product to the packaging spot?

- Is the empty packaging within arm's reach of the operator putting the items in the package?
- Is the package ready to receive the items when the items are ready to go in the package?

Once we felt like we had built the process, we then did some practice with the new process. We put members of the team in each operator's place and ran through the process to see if there was anything we had missed.

As this was happening, every member on the team could see how much less time the revised process was taking. We were all actually doing the process and seeing how quickly it could be done. We also found that 6 operators were too many, and having that many slowed down the process when they were trying to work around each other. Now, we only needed four operators in the main work area most of the time, with support from a fifth operator or Lead to direct the traffic and keep the other four stocked with the necessary supplies to accomplish their packaging tasks.

This fifth operator performed a valuable role. The fifth operator ensured the other four did not have to stop the flow of goods to move the packaged product out and supplies in. That fifth operator could also jump into the process at the constraint to help increase the speed of the process slightly when demand rose.

If we compared the old process functions with the new process functions, the most obvious difference was how much the product was unnecessarily handled before the changes. The old process had almost every operator picking up and setting down product from the floor. Also, the shipping packages were used to move the product through the process, and they were too large for the work area when they started to stack up. We found that we could use stackable trays that we had on hand to help move the product through the new process without taking up too much space.

About 4 months later, one particularly heavy volume day brought 1650 line items of work to the department. On that particular shift, those 5 operators were completely finished and cleaned up in 8-1/2 hours. They then proceeded to move out to other departments to help everyone else finish up.

For the rest of that night and the next day, there was much buzz about how much this little department had done the day before, and then how they helped everyone else!

Volume continued to rise on average, and they tackled many more heavy volume shifts. Many times the operators finished up and moved to other departments to help out for the rest of the shift. In this case, the gains were obviously greater than 10%.

Here is the comparison of before and after.	
Before:	After:
6 operators x 10.5 hours = 63 labor hours	5 operators x 8.5 hours = 42.5 labor hours
1300 lines/63 labor hours = 20.63 lines/hr.	1650 lines/42.5 labor hours = 38.82 lines/hr.

The improvement shown in this case nearly doubled productivity. After a few more months, the process settled in and the process showed more than double the productivity when compared to previous year's data.

This particular project took less than 2 weeks. First week was introduction and getting familiar with what we were going to do and how to do it. Two days into the second week, we were up and running and observing the process.

This kind of improvement wasn't a one-time event. In the course of one year, this particular facility benefited from a 20 to 50% improvement in five different departments. Either the department as a whole or one of the major processes in that department benefited from applying Only-Exactly.

RECEIVING DEPARTMENT – DISTRIBUTION CENTER

Step #1-Picking the Target

The target this time was the receiving of a different company's distribution center. In this case, the Receiving Department was charged with receiving goods and putting them away in their pre-assigned locations. The specific target process was the unloading of full trailer-loads of cases.

The trailers arrived with product stacked from floor to ceiling and from the front of the semi-trailer to the doors. The originating warehouse did this in order to get as much product as possible in one truckload.

There was a reason this process needed to be targeted. Every time a container arrived, it was a serious burden to the Receiving department and to the other departments. When it arrived, Receiving usually found it necessary to borrow 2-3 more operators from another department in order to be able to unload truck before the shipping company began charging for an overstay at the loading dock.

The original process consisted of about 100 feet of conveyor with half of the conveyor motorized. The non-motorized portion of the conveyor (roller conveyor) was used inside the trailer. The motorized conveyor was used to move the cases from the scanning station, just outside the trailer, to the offloading area. The original process entailed two operators loading the roller conveyor in the

truck, one operator at the scanning station, and 2-3 operators offloading.

As the cases were pushed down the conveyor by adding more cases, they would move to the scanning area where they would be scanned into the computer receiving system and a sticker applied to indicate which pallet to put that case on. Then the motorized conveyor would move them into the offloading area where as many as 50 numbered pallets were set out on the floor to load with cases. The cases would move along until they stopped at the end of the conveyor or were picked up in-transit and placed on the corresponding numbered pallet.

Often the cases would stack up and the offloaders would have to walk to the end of the conveyor to grab a case, just to walk back almost to the scanning station to find the correct pallet for that case. There was little room between the pallets and when the conveyor started getting full, it would slow down the loading and scanning areas.

At any given time, one of the three areas were behind which would cause the other two processes to have to slow or stop to wait until they caught up. This meant that 3-4 people were not working at full capacity almost all the time. On rare occasions, the line flowed evenly but never for more than a few minutes.

It would usually take 5 operators 3 hours or 6 operators 2.5 hours to unload a truck. Fifteen labor hours for 1200 cases was considered good. This translated to approximately 75-80 cases per labor hour.

Step #2-Build the Team

Due to the small number of people in the Receiving department, we decided that the whole department should be on the team. This naturally created buy-in from everyone in the department since they would all have a say in the changes. The Supervisor, who had previous experience in Breaking the Box and Only-Exactly, was in-charge of this project.

Step #3-Only-Exactly

This Only-Exactly wasn't quite as easy to get to for the team. It took a couple of meetings of the team to get there since they were trained to believe that the way they had been doing it was the best. After breaking it down, the Supervisor got them to understand that the only thing that must happen was that the truck had to be unloaded. The rest of the steps were things done—facilitating the systems, tracking of goods, and policies of the company—were secondary. Basically, these requirements of the company and the accounting systems weren't part of the Only-Exactly. They finally got the Only-Exactly down to its base statement, "Unload Truck".

Step #4-Rebuild the Process

Now, came the part where they had to figure out what was necessary to the unloading of the truck without the distractions of the company functions they had built into the system. What was simple waste?

Then they could add in the functions that facilitated inventory tracking, etc. They were able to see that they were lifting the cases onto a conveyor so that they could be scanned and put on a pallet. They understood that each case had to be scanned for the tracking, and that it had to be put on a pallet to facilitate the successive processes, namely putting it away where it was supposed to be stored.

Once they understood that these few steps were all that had to happen as the truck was unloaded, they began to realize that the order of those steps were not dependent on each other. This got them thinking.

Eventually the Supervisor helped lead them to ask the question, "Why can't we just put them on pallets and scan them afterward?" This was the breakthrough question. After some debate, they got it down to simply this:

1) 2 operators stack cases from the truck right onto pallets in the back of the truck.
2) 1 operator operates a forklift to move full pallets out and empty pallets in.
3) When the forklift is carrying out a full pallet, the other two are stacking the empty pallet the forklift just brought in.
4) When the truck is empty, one person scans all the cases and applies the stickers while the other two go on to other processes in the department.

Because the cases would no longer be sorted onto pallets to go to the area that each needed to go in the warehouse, there was concern that this would cause extra work. What they found in reality was that the cases were not as mixed up as they expected. Because the trucks were loaded in sections with similar types of product stacked together, sorting was already partially accomplished.

They also noted that during the original put-away process every operator usually spent some time organizing each pallet before moving to put it away. So these changes did not add so much additional labor time to the next process that it would negate the gains made by improving the unloading process.

Another observation helped to justify the change. Each truck brought in product from different companies. All the same brand of product and the similar product types from that brand were generally stored adjacent to each other.

The end result was that three operators could unload 1,200 cases onto pallets in about 1.5 hours. It then took one operator about 2

hours to scan and sticker the cases. Now, they were unloading trucks at the rate of 175-200 cases per hour! The efficiency more than doubled!

They never again had to borrow operators from other departments after these changes were implemented. The trucking companies never again charged for an overstay when the unloading took too long. And the goods were put away and ready for sale hours (and often a full day) sooner than before.

While this project focused on those trucks that were loaded full from floor to ceiling, these changes also changed the process for those loads that came in already on pallets. With these loads, they didn't have to unload them onto pallets. Because they were already palletized, Receiving was usually able to receive those loads even faster. Most times two operators could offload one of those full pallet loads at a rate of over 300 cases per hour!

Considering Effects of Changes Downstream

Of course, when implementing these changes, they also had to consider the effects their changes would have on any processes downstream. If preventing overstay charges resulted in other costs that proved greater, then the change would have been counter-productive.

The put-away process slowed down by about 10-15% at first because the process was slightly different. But once everyone got used to it, the overall drop in productivity was less than 5% and still within the productivity standards which had been in place before the changes in the unloading process were made.

Fortunately, the Receiving department had added incentive to make sure the downstream processes were still viable. They were the ones who were handling most of those processes. They wanted to make sure the new and improved method of unloading trucks did not actually cause their job tasks to become more difficult. They also wanted to make sure their achievements in increasing productivity were not undermined by problems elsewhere in the system.

LARGE VOLUME DISTRIBUTION CENTER

Step #1-The Target

This particular distribution center shipped about 2000–2500 cases/day. The cases were stored in an area of about 120,000 square feet in floor to ceiling racks. The distribution center was laid out much like a supermarket with aisles and on each aisle there were products on both sides in assigned locations from the floor level all the way to the top of the racks near the ceiling.

There were six operators using order picker lifts to pull the cases from their assigned location in the warehouse and load them onto a conveyor that ran along one side of the warehouse, just for this purpose. The goal was to reduce the amount of hours required to pull all the cases in an 8-hour shift.

Step #2-The Team

Initially, the team consisted of the operators and the leadership team from that shift, but we soon found that this project would require support from other departments and shifts in order to maximize its effectiveness.

Step #3-Only-Exactly

The Only-Exactly is this case was simple since the process was relatively uncomplicated: pull (or 'pick') cases. Actually grabbing a case was an easy process. The time/labor spent traveling between 'picks' and the conveyor appeared to be the most time consuming. We were looking at rebuilding a process where the least amount of travel or motion would be involved.

Any movement at all in any direction is waste. We must reduce the movement of all functions, operators, machinery, and product and any combination of these. The micro-logistics of parts of this process are key to most improvements of this type.

Step #4-Rebuilding

To ensure we would be allowing as little movement (waste) as possible, we started at the end of the process and worked backwards. The case being placed on the conveyor was the end of the process so we started there.

The first question we asked was, "Is it possible to have the operator stand at the conveyor and not move in any direction other than to pick up the case and place it on the conveyor?" The answer actually could have been 'yes', if the location of the product was next to the conveyor. So the next question was, "Can we put all products next to the conveyor?" No, since there were about 30,000 different products and there were only a couple hundred feet of conveyor. So we now knew that the operator had to move.

Volume of product (30 thousand) required that products be located throughout the entire warehouse. It took the whole warehouse to store them. We all agreed that all the locations in the warehouse were necessary to store everything.

By this time, we had determined that we could not move the products next to the conveyor since there wasn't enough room to do so. Not to mention that it would be very expensive to move the racks and create another system for storing the product.

We could not move the racks and we also could not move the conveyor since that too would be expensive (Remember the goal of this method is to teach you how to make changes with minimal financial impact to the company). So we started over with our assessment of the situation. This time we wanted to see where all the movement was in the process so we could focus on it.

Note: In many cases, what you (or the team) thinks is happening within a process is not entirely correct. You may be missing some very discrete or important events within the process.

One of the best ways to learn or rebuild a process is to physically walk through every single step of the process or to watch the original operator walk through the process to find out if you have observed and accounted for every little detail of the process.

easiest spot for retrieval?

We decided to walk it through on the floor to observe the process and see what exactly was happening.

The team moved to the floor to watch the process in action. We started with one case at a floor level location. The operator picked up the case label, drove to the location, scanned the case, applied the label, put the case on his machine, drove to the conveyor, and put it on the conveyor.

The team then discussed the process step-by-step.

Step #1: Picking up the label

Were the labels at the closest and

Step #2: Drive to the location

As previously discussed we knew we could not move one product closer without moving another product farther away.

Step #3: Scan the case and apply label

This step involved little movement and was necessary to ensure quality levels.

Step #4: Drive to conveyor

This involved the same amount of time as driving to the location of the product.

Step #5: Putting product on conveyor

This step obviously could not be eliminated and actually involved very little movement.

Most of the team believed that this was one process that was not going to be improved much, until one team member reminded everyone that the operators didn't just pick one case at a time. They picked multiple cases before moving to the conveyor.

One rule of thumb that is rather accurate in business and in life is the Pareto principle, which states that 80% of effects come from 20% of the causes.

We then tested this concept on the floor. First, we observed the process when the operator picked two cases and unloaded them, then three cases, etc. After each test run, we discussed the process. After observing this, one member noticed that if we were able to reduce the movement BETWEEN locations then that could produce a huge improvement.

This raised the question, "How could we reduce the movement between locations?" Someone pointed out that some products sell thousands of cases per month while others only sold one or two cases per month. Could we move those products that sold at higher volumes closer together so the operators traveled less distance between these popular products? This might be the key! The operators were already going to these products more often. Instead of having all the products with the highest velocity scattered all over, if we moved them closer together and closer to the conveyer belt, total travel time would be reduced.

We looked at the Pareto principle and found that it applied. 80% of the volume in the operation came from 20% of the products. So we sat down to figure out how to move the top 20% of the products closer together without increasing the travel for the other 80%.

First we thought that if we moved the top products to those locations closer to the conveyor then that would be enough. So we theoretically moved all the products to the front of the racks closest to the conveyor and drew it out on a large sheet of paper. We made little rectangles to represent the picker lifts and "drove" them from location to location on the paper to observe the movement.

We soon noticed that the time and distance used to drive around a corner to another rack was taking far longer when compared to moving between products within one rack. The next question naturally was, "Can we put ALL 20% in one aisle so the operator pulling the popular cases can stay in one aisle?" The answer was no, but we found that we could put all these products in two aisles.

We drew it out so that all of the most popular items were in two aisles. We then theoretically assigned one operator to each aisle and drove them through the process on paper. What we found was that the two operators could pull 80% of the total volume that went out

each day, and the distance and time needed to travel between products was reduced by up to 90%.

Now the operators could grab the labels, drive to their aisle, pick a product, move a few feet, pick another, and repeat until the machine was full then move straight down the aisle, unload and move straight back into the aisle without ever turning a corner or driving around. We even set it up to where another operator could pick most of the remaining 20% of the volume on the floor level of the warehouse by putting the next most popular products in designated floor locations. (We did this instead of putting the next highest velocity items in a third aisle because there was too many products with a similar velocity and because our equipment traveled faster at floor level.)

It took most of the two weeks to rebuild the process. Once the concept was in place, we found that we did not have the resources to immediately relocate all the products, but we were able to create a process that permanently assigned the fastest moving products to those two aisles over a period of months as inventory was sold off.

Eventually 4 operators were easily doing what it had taken 6 operators to do before.

The key to rebuilding this process was persistence and re-evaluating what was really happening. The reduction was actually the time and movement between each single only-exactly within the process. Often the biggest efficiency gains are between smaller processes and inside a larger system. The micro-logistics of a process are very important.

QUALITY CONTROL DEPARTMENT

Step #1-Picking the Target

This process was a Quality Control point where orders to customers were double-checked for accuracy and packed. This was the last opportunity to catch errors before the customer received the products. The process consisted of comparing each and every item against the order ticket for correct item and quantity. At the time, the Quality Rate was between 98% & 98.5% with a goal of 98.8%.

Step #2-The Team

On this occasion, the team consisted of all the leads, supervisors, and the department manager—all of who had jumped in and worked in this area before when volume was high and the department was running behind.

Step #3-The Only-Exactly

This process had two different functions rolled into one. The first function was the double-checking of the order and then the packing of the order. It had originally been paired up since they could be done simultaneously; the product was checked and put in the shipping box then sealed for shipment. We handled this process with the possibility of looking at it as one process and/or as two separate processes depending on the best way to rebuild it. The Only-Exactly was 'Check and Pack Product'.

Step #4-Rebuilding

Checking in the existing process consisted of taking the product and the order ticket and comparing each order line with the product to make sure they were an exact match for item and quantity. This was done by one operator who grabbed the product and the order ticket

and moved it to a table. Here the operator checked the product and put it in a pile.

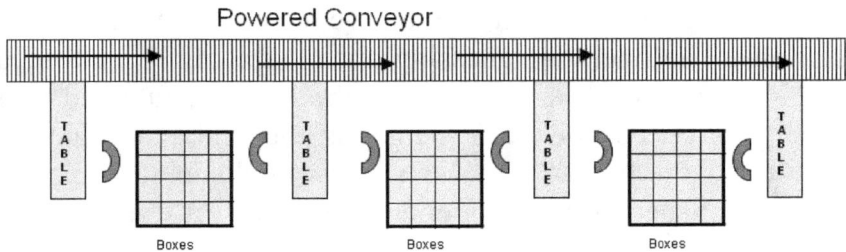

Powered Conveyor

Boxes   Boxes   Boxes

Original Process Layout

The operator then had to find a box of the appropriate size to pack the goods in. Many of the boxes were recycled so there were many different sizes to choose from. It was very difficult to have enough boxes near the tables due to space constraints, and the boxes were not all in one spot. Rather the operator had to walk from table to table to see whether that table had a recycled box on it that would work.

When the operator found a box, the operator would move back to his/her table in order to put the goods in the box. Then the operator would put it on the conveyor adjacent the table.

Rebuild Model #1

We first looked at the process as a whole, looking at the two functions as one. Since all the tables were movable, we had the luxury of actually changing the layout and watching how the operators adjusted to the flow. The first thing we did was move the tables so that most of the boxes were between two tables. The operators were now working with a shared stack of boxes behind them that was twice as large. We hoped the operators would be able to check the goods and pack them right into the box as they checked them.

In order to test this new process, the operators had to find a box before checking the product. What we observed failed to meet expectations. The operator, guessing at the size of the box needed, would try to find one near that size. If the operator guessed wrong, he or she would need to unpack the goods and find a box that fit the order better. If the box was too small, it was difficult to close and had a greater chance of breaking open in transit. If it was too large, it would often be crushed by other boxes in transit.

Additionally, we observed that if the operators were still not able to find boxes to their liking in their stack, they would walk over to other stacks to find a better box. This happened less often than before, but it remained motion that was waste. Most operators were trying to find the BEST box for their order. We did not want to discourage the motivation to find the best for the customer. We would have to rebuild it differently.

Rebuild Model #2

This time we looked at splitting the two main functions of the process between two operators. We worked with the same layout as we tested during our first rebuild, putting two operators on a table, one to check and immediately pass the goods to the second operator who then put the order in a box. It was apparent that this was better since one operator could concentrate on checking the order and the other could concentrate on boxing. This system worked even better when we put two tables end to end to double the length of the work area by providing a buffer between them.

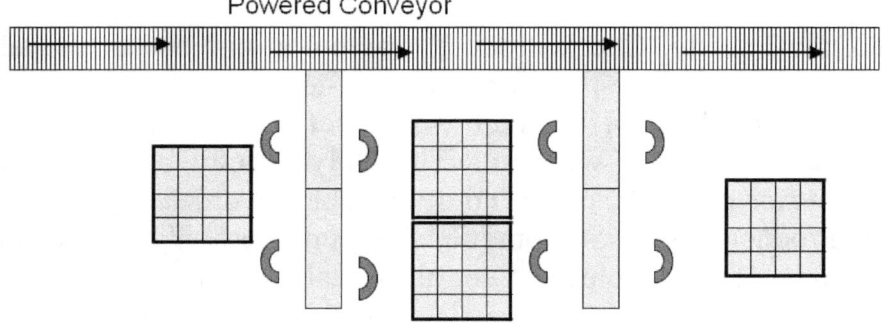

Powered Conveyor

Second Rebuild Layout

It worked better but…

The second operator was still traveling to find a box. The time spent finding a box often slowed the first operator down once the table became crowded with piles of orders. Additionally, sometimes the orders got mixed up which led to more errors rather than preventing them. Traveling to find a box and the stacking up of orders, which then got mixed up, were two things we were not willing to build into the process!

We needed to reduce the travel for a box and prevent the orders from getting mixed up, while making sure nothing slowed down the operator checking the goods. This time we looked at the direction we were seeing progress. We had placed two tables end-to-end, and things had improved. But not enough. So we totally split the two functions.

Rebuild Model #3

The Only-Exactly 'Check Product' was put at one end of the table with one operator. We put four tables end-to-end to provide a buffer so the Check Product operator would not have to stop checking unless all four tables were full. The Only-Exactly 'Pack Product' function was put at the other end of the table. In order to prevent the Pack Product operators from traveling unnecessarily, we created three rows of four tables and set all the tables to flow in the same direction parallel to the conveyor. All the boxes were put at the 'Pack Product' end of the tables.

To ensure the orders would not get mixed together, we cut the top off of the most standard-size box and converted these boxes into transport trays. Not only did these boxes serve to keep the orders separate, they provided the second operator with a visual reference for what size of box would hold the order.

All the available boxes were stacked in one big area adjacent to the end of the tables so that the Pack Product operator never had to travel more than a few feet to find an appropriately sized box. The empty transport trays were easily stacked together. But the Pack Product operators developed an even more efficient system.

The found it was easy to slide the boxes back to the check product operator on the floor beneath the tables. No waste was added at this step, because each time a box was emptied the Pack Product operators would push the row of boxes back toward the Check Product operator with the newly emptied box.

The Check Product operator began checking the order right into the transport trays. When the Check Product operator was finished, he/she pushed it down the table a few feet and began checking the next order. The Pack Product operator would look at the transport

tray, walk a couple of steps, pick an appropriate size box, pack the order, and put it on the conveyor.

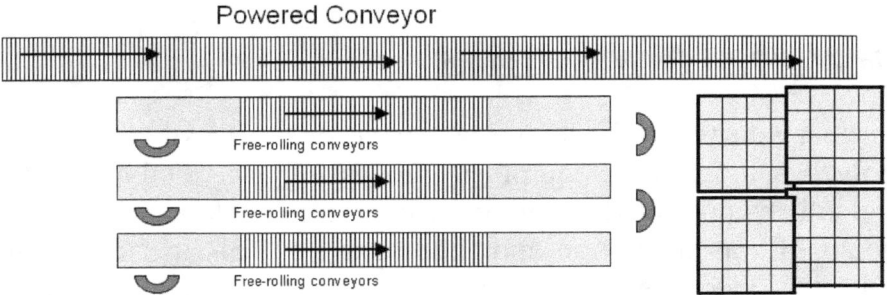

Final Layout

We soon found that switching the middle tables for free-rolling conveyors meant that the Pack Product operators no longer had to travel to get the transport tray. Also, due to the savings in time NOT traveling to find a box, two packing operators easily kept up with the workload that had previously taken three operators to handle.

Another side benefit that reduced costs was the fact that orders were no longer getting mixed together at the checking table. The checking operators were able to focus on checking the product exclusively, and once the check was completed the system was now designed to prevent loss of accuracy after that checkpoint.

Remember the goal was to reach 98.8% accuracy. This goal was exceeded in two months when the quality rate improved to over 99%, despite a reduction in the number of operators handling the process. Within a year it was better than 99.3% and improving.

We found that productivity also increased approximately 20-25% on average. The need for other staff to step in when this department fell behind was significantly reduced. The elimination of the extra travel for the boxes, and the fact that the checking operators no longer had to wait when the packing process backed up were main contributors to this positive outcome.

THE WINDOW MANUFACTURER

The goal you wish to achieve when the operation of equipment is involved is to keep the equipment processing at its Only-Exactly as efficiently as possible by having the operators working with the least amount of wasted motion and time possible. This usually requires timing the operators so they have the input ready exactly when the machine is ready for it and are also handling the output quickly so the machine does not have to wait for output to be cleared.

When the operators make sure the primary Only-Exactlies for a piece of equipment, Input and Output, are handled properly, the equipment will be able to run at full capacity. Anything that gets in the way of the operators achieving their specifics goals in this regard creates pure waste.

The following example shows how a window manufacturer used the principles of Only-Exactly to become more efficient.

Step #1-The Target

The target process was the operation of one piece of equipment, a glass-cutting machine called the optimizer. The optimizer's purpose was to cut sheets of glass in such as way as to get the most residential windows possible out of one sheet of glass. The manufacturer recommended three operators be assigned to the machine for maximum production.

Step #2-The Team

For this project, building a formal team was not needed. This project was done basically on-the-fly and was up and running by the end of the shift.

Step #3-The Only-Exactly

In this instance, the Only-Exactly was actually determined by the purpose of the optimizer. This Only-Exactly was to cut glass. Since this was actually done by the optimizer, the focus of the Only-Exactly shifted to the processes that were handled by the operators while the optimizer was in use. This is typical. For the operators of most processing equipment, the Only-Exactlies are the input and/or output.

The optimizer required operators for both input and output. The input end focused on large stock sheets of glass. The output focused on unloading the cut glass.

Step #4-Rebuilding

The rebuilding in this project was not necessarily the Only-Exactly connected with the optimizer. It was the rebuilding of the Only-Exactlies of the operator(s) to ensure that the equipment could _meet the needs_ of the rest of the manufacturing operation. Three operators ensured running at full capacity, but one question had never been answered. "Did this piece of equipment need to run at full capacity?" How did production fit the needs of the scheduled shifts at the next process?

The output requirements of this piece of equipment (or any equipment that plays a role in an operation) had to be determined before rebuilding the process. This is where team members from downstream departments were most helpful. They had already supplied this information.

The optimizer was designed with three stages in mind; Input, Processing, Output. The input area was a table that held one sheet of stock glass. Processing occurred on a second table. Then a third table became the output area where the glass sheet was broken apart and offloaded. The manufacturer of the machine recommended that one operator work at input and two at output. Of course this assumed that the business needed maximum output to meet the needs of the next department.

This was a box begging to be broken. This was an example of the type of situation where a manager motivated to improve operations needs to look at all processes and challenge the 'recommendations'. After all, recommendations are nothing more than suggestions.

To start rebuilding this process, we had to be careful we weren't falling into the trap of adding resources to the process until we were certain that the recommended amount of resources needed to operate this process/equipment weren't needed to meet the needs of the rest of the operation. If changes in the process met the needs of downstream departments, it didn't matter whether changes fit the manufacturer's recommendations.

In the end, we arranged the process so that one operator handled both input AND output with the minimum amount of movement (micro-logistics) possible. How did we accomplish this? We figured out how long it took for one person to prepare a sheet of glass for processing, then move down to offloading to breakout the cut piece of glass, and then do it all over again.

We refused to add a second operator until we established exactly how much one operator could accomplish on average over the course of an entire 8-hour shift. In this case, it was not difficult to determine how long the optimizer took to complete the actual loading, cutting and moving to the breakout table. The equipment process time varied by only a few seconds from cycle to cycle.

After that, we were able to determine how long it took for only one operator to complete their portion of the cycle—loading a sheet of glass at input, moving to output, and unloading the cut glass. As expected, the equipment could complete a cycle faster than it took the operator to complete a cycle. However, it only took 20 seconds longer than the optimizer for the operator to complete his cycle.

Now we could figure out how many cut pieces one operator could produce on this equipment in one 8-hour shift. We took this number and compared it with how many pieces were actually needed by the next step in the manufacturing process. We found that for that process, only ONE operator was necessary to keep up with the demand of the next manufacturing process. When and if the next process demanded more than what one operator could produce on the optimizer, then we would look at how we would rebuild the process or how to add labor hours without adding waste.

As a side note, two of the operators originally on the equipment were thrilled to be able to move to other areas in manufacturing and learn other processes. The operator now handling the equipment solo was proud that he was able to do the same amount of work it had formerly taken three operators to accomplish.

MORE BREAKING THE BOX IN REAL LIFE

Now that you have the basic premise of how to "break the box" in the real workplace, it's time to see what it looks like to break the box in different scenarios. Here we haven't focuses on the steps.

When looking at a department or process to improve, you typically will want to find the key process within the target department, or the process that requires the most time resource.

HANDLING CUSTOMER RETURNS

In a real-life example, a large corporation operated a number of very high-volume distribution centers. Like most distribution centers or warehouses, they also handled the customer returns for their products at that same distribution center. This corporation had a standard of being no more than three days behind on processing customer returns.

Three days?? Time to break a box.

I soon found out that all of the distribution centers within this corporation had 2 to 3 days worth of return inventory waiting to be processed. The amount of inventory tied up with 12 distribution centers holding three days worth of customer returns was in the millions of dollars.

First, I defined the goal. I wanted to reduce the amount of inventory tied up in customer returns. This would free up this inventory to be resold or appropriately handled, as well as providing the customer with the credit back as quickly as possible, leading to happier customers.

We were not looking to just reduce from three days down to one or two days; we are looking to ultimately use as few MINUTES as possible from the time the customer returns arrived until they were processed.

The concept to understand in this case was that the amount of labor required to remain three days behind was exactly the same amount of labor required to remain zero days behind. It was still one day's work whether we did it three days later or on the day the returns arrived.

So what was our Only Exactly? In this case, it was simple, Process Returns. However, it was so simple that the team had a difficult time understanding the concept of an Only-Exactly. They all knew that they Processed Returns. That was their job, so I asked them to break the process down to the least amount of steps. I asked them to write down the minimum steps necessary to Process Returns if they were at their work station and had EVERYTHING they needed sitting right there in front of them.

This helped them to understand that doing only what was absolutely necessary to Process Returns at their workstations was their Only-Exactly.

The procedure for customer returns indicated that the item had to be matched up with a previous purchase from that customer. A scan of the barcode on that item after the proper customer returns screen had been accessed on the database accomplished the match-up requirement.

So the team decided the Only-Exactly for each returns processing operator came down to three things.

1. Open customer returns screen to the right customer.
2. Scan barcode and enter condition and amount.

3. Put item in correct box/location for return to inventory or other handling.

That's it. The rest of the steps in the returns process fell under micro-logistics.

So now that we knew the three steps to accomplish our Only-Exactly of Processing Returns, our next step was to completely map the existing present process by steps and compare to see whether there was any waste.

Since this process involved such a large portion of the department and because many of the operators spent all of their work hours within this process, we brought them into the improvement phase. We wrote down all of the steps in the process that we were currently doing on paper and attached magnetic strips on the back. Each step was written on its own magnetic strip. We stuck the strips on the metal file cabinet right by the entrance/exit of the department.

The operators rearranged the steps on the file cabinet until they had established an order that allowed the process to be completed with the least amount of steps. As they did this, they quickly noticed that some of the steps where very redundant and were completely unnecessary. After a few days, the whole department went over the process step-by-step. The result was that they reduced the whole process to the smallest number of steps and still met all the needs of the process.

The final piece of the Only-Exactly was to establish what the final process would look like.

- Move one pallet of customer returns to each customer returns specialists work area
- Pick up one box and open it.
- Open the proper customer returns screen.
- Find the correct customer.

- Pickup each item in box and scan the barcode into the system.
- Put item in the appropriate box for return to inventory or other handling.

Now, we had to put it into practice.

The goal for the second week of this project was to be zero days behind by the end of the week. Everyone understood this and was on board. So on Monday morning, we begin by using the new process on the returns that had just arrived that day. After that day's returns were processed, we began to work on the returns that were three days old.

I expected to be completely caught up sometime Friday afternoon. Surprisingly, just after noon on Thursday we were completely caught up and finished with every customer return in the building. We had completed seven days worth of customer returns in 3 3/4 days. From that point on, all customer returns were completed within a few hours of arriving at the distribution center. In less than two weeks, we had set a new standard. We had also benefited the company by introducing significant labor savings, shrink reduction, increased customer satisfaction, and reduced inventory expenditure due to the increased inventory available for sale.

BREAKING THE CUBICLE

The customer call center needed a quick boost in productivity with little to no added labor expense. Now, in a cubicle environment the processes are different. Since this is an environment driven by human behavior, we look for the opportunity in areas with a focus on micro-logistics.

In this particular office, the call center called current customers to discuss their account. Much like sales, this was a numbers game where more calls equaled more productivity/results. What we found

was that the Only-Exactly was the phone call, or in other words, communication. The more phone calls and the better the communication, the better the results.

So where was the waste? What prevented the call center operators from more phone calls with better communication?

Often a customer had questions about their account that was not readily available in the computer system. This meant the call center operator left his or her desk to retrieve the file. This provided an opportunity for extended time not calling or communicating. When multiple operators were retrieving files, the factor of socializing magnified exponentially.

In this case, the improvement was rather simple and was implemented the next day. One person pulled the files needed for the next day's calls. The hours needed to organize and pull the files were easily offset by the number of minutes divided out between all the call center operators who had been retrieving files. Essentially one person retrieved multiple files in one trip. Socializing during regular work time was minimized, the file room was kept better organized along with the files, and the call center operators always had the best information for the customer almost instantly. More calls and more communication with better information led to better results in productivity.

BREAKING THE BOX ON AN ASSEMBLY LINE

An assembly line or production line is different in that the order of the process is very important; however, there are improvements to be found.

Due to the nature of a production or manufacturing line, where small processes are closely tied to the processes immediately preceding and following each process, very minor changes in a process can significantly impact productivity and efficiency. Any time lost in manufacturing is potential productivity lost forever.

However, one "process" that can most impact productivity of an assembly line is not really a process per se. In a standard eight-hour shift, operator typically can only be productive for 7.5 hours due to rest breaks. Many manufacturing facilities miss this important fact. In addition, lunchtime, which is not part of paid productivity time, is also lost time in a manufacturing line. In an 8.5 hour shift counting the lunch break, there is a full hour of lost time.

The best way to take advantage of this lost time is to find the one or two processes that are the bottleneck or constraints of your production line and arrange your labor hours to keep those processes working during those lunch and rest breaks. In most cases, it is possible to create enough buffer before and after the constraint process in the production line to facilitate that process being productive for the full 8-1/2 hours. If you are not already taking advantage of your breaks and that time available, this should provide a 10 to 15% increase in your productivity.

Applying the Lunch and Break Factor

This overlooked improvement opportunity—taking advantage of lunches and breaks to elevate the constraint and bring an instant improvement in productivity to the operation—is where we slip in the Theory of Constraints as a tool that complements our Only-Exactly process. The basic idea is to use excess capacity in other processes in the assembly to provide labor to the constraint during lunches and breaks.

In a normal 8-hour shift, there is typically an 8.5-hour schedule footprint due to the half hour lunch. In those 8.5 hours, there are usually 2 breaks that range from 10-15 minutes depending on your

company's policies or your local employment law. This translates to only 7.5 hours of actual production time for your assembly line.

For example, let's look at a simple assembly line that has four primary sequential processes. The entire assembly line produces at a rate of 120 units per hour when running. At this rate for 7.5 hours you produce about 900 units per shift on average (120 x 7.5 = 900).

As a motivated manager, you decide to take advantage of the available time during lunches and breaks to increase productivity. You carry out some time studies to determine which of the four primary processes is the constraint. You find that processes #1 and #4 are capable of 200 units per hour and process #2 is capable of 150 units/hr. This leaves process #3 as the constraint at 120 units/hr. This is the process that is limiting production.

The capacity in order would look like this: 200-150-120-200. In reality, every process has a capacity of only 120/hr. because your slowest process of 120 slows down the maximum capacity for each of the other processes.

Elevating the Constraint

In order to resolve this bottleneck, you need to move operators from the other faster processes to the constraint during lunches and breaks so that process #3 does not continue to limit production for the full 8.5 hours. To map this, you will need to stagger the lunches and breaks from the fastest processes to cover process #3. Since process #4 is much faster than process #3, the easiest solution would be to have operators from process #4 move to cover process #3 when process #3 operators go on break and lunch.

Applied successfully, this strategy should soon have the assembly line producing 1020 units/shift (13.33% improvement). To assure success, you will need to ensure there is enough buffer between process #3 and #4 to handle one full hour of work-in-progress (WIP) while the 30-minute lunches are occurring for both sets of operators. Most contract agreements do require lunch breaks to start between four and five hours into the shift so you have 1-1/2 hours that you have to account for all four processes not being at maximum production.

If there is only space available for, let's say, 60 units, then you would need the operators from process #1 to come to either process #3 or #4 to cover for one of the lunches, in which case you need to have room for 60 units of WIP between process #1 and #2 to keep process #2 producing at a rate of no less than 120 units/hr. The ultimate goal is to keep process #3 producing non-stop for the entire 8.5-hour shift with no added labor hours.

Depending on your processes and operation, it can be a bit complicated until you get it nailed down and running smoothly. However, even if you only manage a 10% increase in productivity for those processes, that is an incredible accomplishment when you consider you have not added one single labor hour to your operation.

These examples demonstrate that rapid improvements can be made on a process-by-process basis by using the Only-Exactly method. Choose a process in the production line that is important or happens to be a constraint/bottleneck and break it down to the Only-Exactly. Zero in on what needs to happen at that process.

In some cases, that particular process can be improved on by looking at the micro-logistics of the person or persons performing the process. Bring all necessary parts, tools, and resources to within arm's reach or a half-step away if possible.

Decision-Making for Balance

One dimension of process improvement that cannot be overlooked is balance in the operation or system. Much like an ecosystem, a business must have balance on many levels, or it will not be able to sustain itself for long. There are "macro" balance factors that must be considered when making decisions in a business, like labor hour dollars as a percentage of sales or volume, or purchasing of raw materials based on sales forecasting.

The same is true when making process improvements within an operation, a manufacturing line, or even a single process. But motivated managers approach balance with a slightly different perspective and usually on a smaller scale than the typical number cruncher.

In an operation, making a change in one process can have an effect that ripples to other processes or departments. The goal is to make improvements that either have a net positive effect on the rest of the operation after factoring in the gain in the target process. Or if there is a negative effect, you want to keep its impact minimal so it does not cancel or negate the original improvement.

This can be a complex problem, especially when other departments and other managers are affected by the changes you make in your department's operation. Some process improvement changes may be so broad that they affect those outside of your organization as well. When this is the case, you must ensure all improvements are solid business decisions before moving forward. This is one reason that Six Sigma and other methods may take months and years to complete. They often have to try to take into consideration the impact on each and every department and process within the organization before moving ahead with the changes.

Only-Exactly Advantage

Focusing on improvements that have little to no effect on other departments or operations within your organization will limit the scope of your projects, but this is not necessarily a negative. Keeping the projects manageable and focused will ensure they do not become too big to handle in two weeks and will help to keep you and your team on track. You are not trying to change the business model; you are simply making improvements.

The reason for keeping Only-Exactly projects focused and limited within a 2-week time frame is to help you keep balance in your operation or department. This is also why you, the motivated manager, are in the perfect spot to do this. You have the authority to get things done in your department or facility, as well as the standing/rank to get the needed information from other departments to ensure the least impact elsewhere.

Another important perspective of balance is awareness of the goals and metrics of the organization, notably the performance metrics. Most organizations use some form of metric to measure Productivity and another to measure Quality. These two metrics often directly influence each other, most typically through an inverse relationship. The simplest example of this inverse relationship is observed when a process is being pushed to improve productivity, resulting in a drop in the quality of output from that process. Your goal when seeking results from a process improvement project is to improve on of these metrics without negatively impacting the other in some way. This is where good decision-making is paramount.

PRODUCTIVITY VS. QUALITY

Let's look at an example that pits these two factors against each other. This is an example of an Only-Exactly project that could take 2 weeks or less to get to the solution. Implementing the solution could end up taking weeks or months to attain because of the need to balance in the entire organization.

In this example, we will just use two metrics to demonstrate the challenge, and then expand the example to include other factors that should be considered when determining the value of potential improvements. We will use Units per Hour (UPH) to represent Productivity and Defect Rate Percentage (DRP) to represent Quality.

Your newly assigned department processes and ships about 7500 soccer balls per day on one shift. UPH will be the number of soccer balls labeled per hour and DRP will be percentage of soccer balls with incorrectly applied labels. The minimum standard for a Print-Label operator labeling soccer balls is 40 UPH with a DRP of 0.4% (or 1 defect per 250 units labeled). To ensure consistency, all defects reported by customers are also charged back to the Print-Label operators to apply to their DRP.

About 50% of all soccer balls processed are double-checked for Quality by the next process in your department called C&P (checking and packaging). In this example, the C&P operators are checking to make sure the correct labels are completely adhered to the surface and aligned correctly. Many years ago, the 50% double-check was instituted to improve Quality and to track the quality performance of the Print-Label operators. With this configuration, the actual defect rate to the customer is about 0.2%, which has been standard for the department and the organization. (Since the double-check is a function of another human operator, there is still about a 5% chance that a double-checked unit is actually defective.) The Print-Label operators are averaging 43 UPH overall with a 0.375%

DRP, both just inside the minimum standards. Most Print-Label operators are just barely making both standards and a few are really struggling. A few top performing operators are in the 45 UPH and 0.32% DRP range.

The C&P operators can process 50 UPH when checking and packaging and can process 100 UPH when just packaging, this averages out to 75 UPH. The average demand for any given day is 7500 soccer balls. This means your department requires about 24 Print-Label operators and 12 C&P operators with most everyone in the department getting a few hours overtime every week.

In a standard 8-hour shift, each operator actually only has approximately 7.5 hours of actual productive time. There are two 15-minute breaks each shift. This information is important is because you need to know what the actual productivity is without breaks. When breaks are not accounted for when establishing productivity for an operator, it can lead to misinformation.

Using 7.5 hours as 'Worked Hours' gives a clearer picture of the process. In a very high volume operation, with three shifts a day adds up to 1.5 hours or 6.25% per day of unproductive time. When this isn't accounted for, it is very significant in a very high volume operation.

Each operator knows that they must process more than 300 units per day to meet the standard and that they do not want more than one defect per day to stay well within the quality standard.

You are now the manager of this department and these two main functions. Unit Processing and C&P essentially make-up your entire department. As a motivated manager, you have been tasked with improving the performance of your department, and you are determined to succeed. You understand that just barely maintaining the minimum standards in your newly assigned department is not

going to be acceptable. That is what the last manager of this department accomplished, and that is probably why you're the new manager.

For a week or so you observe the processes and evaluate the flow of the operation. You talk to the department Supervisors, Leads, and operators who tell you without hesitation that when the Print-Label operators increase speed to improve their UPH, their DRP worsens and they move over 0.4% quickly. When they work on improving their DRP, their UPH falls below expectations. The tenuous balance of UPH and DRP (Productivity vs. Quality) are at the heart of the processing operation and its performance. What will you do and still maintain a balance of Productivity and Quality from your department?

First, Break the Box. The target is your department. Your team is all the Supervisors, Leads, and a few operators from each area. You introduce them to the methods you will use to tackle this challenge and soon determine that the Only-Exactly is 'Print-Label Units'. Everything else is essentially waste. But you and your team also know that Quality is very important. You must find a balance when rebuilding, or you may become the new 'last manager'.

Before you proceed, it is time to make sure that you and your team are actually on track to Break the Box. What assumptions or limitations have you and your team brought to the problem? In other words, what do you think you are really trying to accomplish with Productivity and Quality? You know that the Only-Exactly is 'Print-Label Units'. What are you assuming about everything else?

At this point, you may be wondering how this is important to 'balancing the process'. It is incredibly important because you must first ensure that the balance you seek in the operation is focused on those items that really matter. You need to really know what this department should be accomplishing before you can achieve the correct balance.

You've helped the team determine that the Only-Exactly is 'Print-Label Units' and Quality is one of the most important factors that must be considered when rebuilding the process. Now the team decides to collect data about the process by determining the boundaries of the process. This is good information to have, and it prompts the team members to begin to understand the process better, so you let them move ahead with this step.

First, they figure out the answer to the following questions: "How fast can one operator label units with no regard for DRP?" "How slow does one label operator become when that operator strives for 100% quality without regard for UPH." After some actual hands-on testing and calculations, the team is surprised to discover that one operator can process about 100 UPH on average! They also note that the operator labeling at that speed had a DRP of 2.0%, 5 times worse than standard. Conversely, for perfect quality, they find that one label operator striving for perfection has to pace himself or herself at approximately 25 UPH to achieve zero defects.

With this information the team starts working with different scenarios to try to overcome the deadlock of UPH vs. DRP. That is when you decide to stop and remind them that the focus of the project is the entire department. The Only-Exactly is 'Print-Label Units,' thus Only-Exactly is not limited to the single process. The combination of both C&P and Print-Labeling Units ultimately are part of a larger process, which also has the very same Only-Exactly.

The team members have started to limit themselves to the single process and do not realize that they had assumed the one process is the only important factor.

It is time to make sure that the team knows exactly what 'Productivity' and 'Quality' actually mean as it relates this department's goals.

Productivity: This department processes on average, about 7500 units per shift with about 300 operator labor hours per day (counting C&P) or 25 units per labor hour. That is the ACTUAL productivity for this department.

Quality: This department's Quality rate is 0.2% defect rate to the customer. That is the ACTUAL Quality rate for this department. These two factors are what the team should be working on to balance. UPH and DRP are internal measurements used to define one process, and in this case, these are the main components of the 'box' that needs to be broken.

Armed with this new perspective, the team begins to see a whole new picture. The C&P process is part of the Only-Exactly, so those resources can be utilized to create the balance between the two actual important metrics of the department. They realize that if they move the percentage of units double-checked to 100% that it would allow the Print-Label operators to be able to significantly improve their rate of processing units. Aiming for 0.2% as a customer defect rate and knowing that the C&P catches 95% of defects, this means the Print-Label operators could have approximately 10 defects per shift! That is a 4.0% DRP and everyone knows that 100 UPH is possible with 2.0% DRP.

Everyone on the team realizes that the Print-Label operators can now process units as fast as possible and still improve quality to the customer significantly. The team gets excited and puts together the best scenario for the actual performance of the department balancing Units Processed vs. Customer Defect Rate. With a production level of 100 UPH, the department only needs 75 hours of Print-Label operator hours or 10 operators. The C&P now needs 150 hours of operator labor to perform C&P on 100% of the soccer balls produced or 20 operators.

This translates your department's ACTUAL Productivity into 7500 units per shift with 225 operator labor hours or 33.3 units per labor hour and the ACTUAL Quality rate of 0.1% defect to the customer. That's approximately 13,000-14000 labor hours saved annually. Not to mention, unnecessary overtime should become nearly extinct.

Typical Shift			
	Before	After	Difference
P/L Hours	187.5	75	-90
P/L Operators	25	10	-15
C&P Hours	90	150	+60
C&P Operators	12	20	+8
Total Worked Hours	277.5	225	-52.50
Total Hours Paid	296	240	-56
Dept. UPH*	27.0	33.3	*Worked UPH
Dept. DRP	0.40%	2.00%	
Dept. DTC**	0.22%	0.10%	**DTC=Defects to Customer

The table above shows numerically the changes in the structure mentioned above. I added total hours paid so that you could see that by lowering headcount, even more labor hours would be saved since the number of actual breaks is reduced for the overall department.

Here is where balance becomes extremely important. You must make sure the department doesn't capsize under the weight of this epiphany. Maintaining balance must now be your chief concern. You probably have support within the department, with the exception that some operators are wondering if they will lose their jobs. This isn't the only factor to consider.

What cannot be overlooked is the impact this sudden change will have on the department from an external perspective. This is especially important if the UPH and DRP are reported to anyone other than you as performance metrics. From an external perspective it would appear that the DRP skyrocketed. The percent of defective units increase 10-fold and C&P labor hours increased 67%, and you end up with six or seven operators with little to do.

Generally managers and/or directors will become increasingly nervous when even one reported internal performance metric starts heading south for any reason.

At this point, it is very important for you to plan a course of action to get from here to there with minimal negative repercussions. You must balance the moves in your department at a pace the rest of the organization can move with and be comfortable. To deal with this you will want to slowly begin the changeover and address every potential issue with a course of action.

One factor that should be considered is whether this department has been limiting the growth potential of the company. For example, has the sales department been fearful of pursuing more contracts/sales because throughput from this department was the bottleneck? Or could there be other bottlenecks within the system that would be aggravated by increased throughput from your department. If so, you may encounter resistance (to be discussed in another chapter).

You will find that some improvement projects will take you in a direction where you will be able to increase your throughput in addition to improving efficiency. This is typically the case when a department's processes are largely handled by equipment or machines. Most equipment has set cycle times for processes and operators often have stations they must occupy to oversee the operation of equipment. This situation often limits improvements in labor hours which means improvements are gained in throughput.

However, this can also become a delicate situation. If your department has been the bottleneck or constraint for your entire operation this can lead to some other problems that you will need to be aware of. As a bottleneck, your department is the pace car for the whole operation. When the pace is altered, it can wreak havoc with just about every other department in the system.

Even if your department is not the bottleneck, you can still create trouble when throughput is altered. Sales, purchasing, and downstream departments are the most affected. The Sales department has been structured to sell at a certain capacity and will sometimes have trouble adjusting quickly. Either they will not trust that the increased throughput will continue, or they suddenly need to try to push more product into the market.

Meanwhile, purchasing needs to be updated on the changes so that they can purchase according to your projections. If the lead time on raw materials is measured in weeks, you could run out of work before the vendor can catch up to demand.

And most impacted are those departments immediately following your department. They may not be able to handle the increased supply from your department on short notice.

This means that in most cases, you will want to focus your improvements on increasing efficiencies within your own department. If you find that you can increase throughput significantly, then proceed first by communicating to all affected parties, especially upper management and Sales. If oversupply from your department affects market prices, your improvements might not be very welcome.

Whenever you can, keep the projects focused on improving productivity and efficiencies within your department. Much like the improvements that significantly affect reported metrics, use good business sense when moving forward with improvements that significantly alter throughput.

In addition to considering bottlenecks, there are other strategies that should be considered before you implement the plan the team has worked out. For instance, you may begin by lobbying your managers to start using the external customer defect rate as the metric for department quality instead of using the internal DRP as the measuring metric. Suggest moving your department to an overall productivity rate to capture all labor hours in the metrics.

To support your request bring historical data to show where the department has been tracking in the past for this new metric. Address the potential increased defects by incrementally adjusting the UPH in order to track the cause or source of defects. 1) Are the defects of a nature that they make the unit unusable? 2) Or are they issues that are easily fixed by sending the unit back to the first station in the department. Determine the validity of the defects or ascertain the possibility of recycling the units for another value-added purpose.

Another way to handle this is to do multiple smaller Only-Exactly projects on the individual processes or even the C&P and Print-Label processes separately with the goal in mind of transitioning to the new structure. This way you can show many little successes and gain the trust of upper management in your methods. Eventually you could make the leap to the new structure or transition slowly depending on which method you feel will be better received by all parties.

Don't forget the operators that may be lacking hours eventually. A slow, steady changeover will usually allow for natural attrition, or you may be able to transition operators into part-time operators or train them with additional skills.

These decisions and challenges are integral part of being a motivated manager. Best of all, they are the kinds of problems and challenges in your operation you want to have.

When projects have unexpected and potentially sudden upsides or even when a small targeted process needs a little attention, it is very important to keep your operation in balance as much as possible. Between upper management, operators, performance metrics, and your customers, you will have to carefully plot a course to bring everyone along so they will all be there with you to celebrate the win.

Occasionally, the solution keeps on trending and you and your operation can reap the benefits for fiscal years to come. Using the example above, the operators now have a good idea what is important and have a better perspective on what the department is trying to accomplish. This applies to the management as well.

With this knowledge, the whole department can now make decisions based on the key goals of the department. As the operators master their processes, they too can do small things to improve the metrics they are responsible for. All operators in the department can now be 100% accountable for quality in both the Print-Label and C&P processes since all errors are being accounted for either in C&P for the Print Label operators or at the customer level for the C&P operators.

When daily decisions are made with the correct key goals in mind, gradual operator generated improvement will often bring steadily increasing results year over year. In contrast, when a department is focusing on metrics that do not truly reflect the important aspects of the market or do not adequately cover all processes, loopholes

develop which hinder progress. Decisions follow that drive the department away from continuous improvement and success. Only-Exactly projects help to reveal the truly important elements that drive your department incrementally in the right direction.

BALANCE AND JUSTIFICATION

Another important factor in process improvement comes down to simple math. Do the improvements create a net positive value to the bottom line? In other words, do the <u>dollar gains</u> in the project outweigh the <u>dollar costs</u>? As mentioned before, your goal is to do the Only-Exactly improvements with zero out of pocket costs, but often there are other costs that may not be immediately apparent. Sometimes the costs are apparent but overlooked when the improvements receive a lot of positive attention or appear fantastic at first glance.

Context is everything. For instance, in the UPH/DPR example we shared, the potential remodeling of the department operator structure might not have been unattainable if the actual dollar cost of each unit were in the hundreds or thousands, rather than in the dollar range as it would be for a soccer ball.

For example, an operation that was producing circuit boards could not accept a higher defect rate as any defective units would lose all value. But the scenario could be quite different if the end product were a fully assembled computer. Defects might in this case be repairable.

If the cost for each unit is just a couple of dollars, then the labor dollars saved would easily cover the dollars lost in defects. The value of every aspect of the project should be converted to dollars to ensure there is a net positive dollar gain. An improvement in one facility may not be an improvement in another location if the cost of a labor hour is higher or if the local tax structure penalizes the business for something in one state and it's handled differently in another state.

This balance and justification of dollars comes into play in almost every project targeted and is one of the most important factors in all of continuous improvement. After all, businesses exist to make money. If the improvement does not actually produce a net positive effect on the bottom line, **directly or indirectly**, it doesn't really provide a direct improvement.

That's not to say that there aren't improvements you can target that impact the more intangible expenses a business faces. For example, things like training and practice improve efficiency. Some process improvement projects could affect the bottom line positively by reducing liabilities. Targeting practices that take safety considerations into account can be worthwhile.

What you must realize when you apply Only-Exactly to these intangibles, you will often receive very little recognition, if any for them. As a motivated manager, it is up to you to determine the value of change in these instances. Some things are worth doing, not for recognition, but for their intrinsic value to the overall culture of the workplace.

Quality Metrics

Whether you should limit process improvement projects to those that create a net positive effect upon the bottom line can be a subject of debate where Quality is concerned. A rule of thumb to follow in any improvement project you are contemplating is that Quality to the (internal or external) Customer within that process should be increased best case, or remain at previous levels, worst case.

There are a few instances where the metrics of Quality are misappropriated, mismeasured, or misaligned. That is where you, as

a manager, are in the best position to correct the issue and to move ahead with the targeted improvement.

When breaking the box on quality, the first factor to investigate is whether the quality metrics that your operation employs are, in fact, actual measurements based upon the expectations of your customers. In many cases, the metrics used to 'measure' quality are outdated, based upon data that is subjective, or are measuring situations beyond the control of your processes or immediate operation.

Outdated metrics would include holding old standards to new or improved processes. For example, Product 'A' is made with an adjustable latch to help technicians with installation of 'A' into Product 'B' in the field. This is part of a new onsite installation program just initiated by the Sales Department. Quality standards dictate all Product 'A' parts produced must have all latches tightened to ensure proper fit into the established tolerances for Product 'B' when 'A' and 'B' were built as complete units in the factory.

In the new process, tightening the latches before they are sent to the field technicians creates an issue where the latch strength is weakened after the latch on Product 'A' has to be loosened then retightened. If the Quality standards are not updated immediately, everyone loses, especially the customer.

Quality metrics that are based upon data that has to be interpreted subjectively will deliver exactly what is expected of the metric. The metrics can be interpreted in a way that allows them to meet quality requirements.

These are the most dangerous type of metrics to use. Examples of these would include aesthetic flaws, precise minute measurements done with hand tools and the human eye, tactile feedback like rough or smooth, or any other type of judgment based upon human sensory interpretation. You want to try to design internal Quality standards to be able be a simple objective pass/fail where you can.

Another common Quality metric that is detrimental to your business is using quality metrics that measure events or situations beyond the control of the processes and then acting upon this data. For instance, the company's purchasing department finds that they can lower supply costs by using a part that is made from recycled plastic instead of virgin plastic. The recycled part has exactly the same specifications as established by the engineering department but, due to over-processing of the recycled plastic, the part shows a tendency to fail four times as often as the virgin plastic part.

The failure is assigned to the assembly processes since all part and product failures are counted against, and attributed to, the production and assembly processes. Consequently, business decisions and changes are made in the assembly processes in an attempt to rectify the issue, when the actual quality issue originated in the purchasing and engineering processes.

As a motivated manager, these can be tricky problems to solve, but identifying these issues is very important to improving your operation and your business. The best Quality metric in almost every case is long-term customer satisfaction.

At the same time, be careful not to set the bar high on areas of quality that the customer doesn't care about. Design your Quality Program to achieve what the customer believes is high quality, any more and you may be wasting precious resources to impress no one. When the decisions are made in the name of quality, ensure that ultimately it is a win-win for both the customer and your business.

Intangibles That Matter

There are other intangibles that weigh on the outcome of improvements. For instance, company image, company culture,

impact on operator schedules or morale, laws and policy gray areas, and potential liabilities should be investigated for their impact on the business, workforce, and the customers before proceeding. Usually you will be working on small-scale processes but these concerns can come into play.

Two of the most common aspects of any operation that are ripe for improvements that mean dollars to the bottom line are labor hours (with overtime) and increased production. Remember to watch for ANY downside in the improvement and be able to justify any additional costs or dollars lost when figuring the ultimate value of the project. It's up to you to get all the information on the project and make sure the VALUE is there, otherwise, it's not an improvement.

Obviously, the ultimate goal of continuous improvement is to successfully improve the operation. First, you must know what "an improvement" is for your particular operation or particular process and, second, you must know the degree of improvement achieved from the project. Only then can you know if you met the goal. Without establishing the starting point and the end result, you cannot know when an improvement has been successful.

When picking your first target, you will want to pick a target with the highest degree of impact for the least amount of risk. The impact may be in labor dollars saved, higher productivity numbers, better customer satisfaction, quality goals exceeded, and/or a looming issue within the operation that your managers wish to have eliminated. A combination of these is best.

If you are lucky enough to have autonomy, with responsibility only to a set of performance metrics, or if you are the owner of your business, you are in a position to achieve incredible results. The only limitations you really have are those set by law, company policy, and professional ethics. If you have to answer to a local chain of command, your challenges may be more complex. You will need to be mindful of their perceptions and fears.

IDENTIFYING THE BASELINE

To determine what would have the most positive impact on the operation and the biggest boost to the image of the program, the best thing to do is ask your manager. If the answer is generic, like "Everything is equally important," take notice of what he/she talks or asks about the most often. If the issue is not a problem in your managers' eyes, then it has little value right now. Save that target for another time.

After noting the topics discussed most often by your managers, look at the metrics your managers are using to determine whether the operation is meeting performance expectations. Any target you choose that has a positive impact that can be directly attributed to your project is great.

Basically, pick targets first that will have the most impact on those issues or metrics your managers care the most about. If you feel you have to build their confidence in your efforts, this is a key factor.

IDENTIFYING THE IMPROVEMENT

Now that you know what targets to choose first, how will you know when your project is successful? If it noticeably improves one of the metrics and you can directly attribute the improvement to your project, then it is a success. For those who wish to work with hard numbers, any improvement that is a quantifiable as greater than 5% is a success.

Why only 5%? For a 2-week project, with no out-of-pocket costs, 5% is a success. If your first target happened to be a constraint in the operation, you are essentially increasing productivity for the whole operations 5% in 2-weeks. If you stack 5% multiple times in a year within an operation on a metric like reduced overtime, the dollar savings are significant. All those saved labor dollars go straight to the bottom line.

5% is modest and successful. 10-15% is great. Celebrate big when the process improvement project shows 25% or more. If you are a large operation, this could equal MILLIONS of dollars annually in profit. For many very large corporations, a ONE percent improvement could mean TEN OF MILLIONS to the bottom line.

Another easy rule of thumb is this. Anytime you send dollars to the bottom line, declare success.

In order to determine a quantifiable improvement, be sure to have data that shows the past history of the target processes. Without quantifiable data, your improvements may be real, but they are just hearsay until you can quantifiably prove they exist. Always compare apples to apples and know that no data is perfect, but imperfect data compared to data with the same imperfections is still acceptable data.

For example, avoid comparing things like internal Quality rates (like manufacturing defects) with external Quality rates (customer feedback or complaint tracking). These are completely different, even though both are important.

HAVING REALISTIC IMPROVEMENT EXPECTATIONS

Another pitfall is expecting to see immediate results from your process improvement. Remember that the operators are often learning or relearning how to complete the process. They are experts of the old method and have to master the new method. Especially with a major process change, it may take a week or more after the initial 2-week project for them to make it their own.

Sometimes, they will suggest small adjustments to the process. Pay attention to these suggestions as they may be inadvertently reversing the improvements or, best case, they are catching a detail that was overlooked by the team and will further improve the process.

Sometimes the process improvement will continue to improve for months and even years. Defect and quality rates are a few of the most common metrics that can continue to positively trend for months after a project is completed.

What you will find is that your most successful projects will see a 50%, or even 100%, improvement in that process for one aspect of that process. Your labor hours may be halved, the defect rate may drop 90%, the overtime could be completely eliminated, or you could even make one of the organization's metrics become obsolete.

I have seen one instance when an Only-Exactly project essentially eliminated a performance metric from the operation. Remember the Customer Returns example? This metric followed the number of days it took for each time-sensitive product to clear the targeted process. Typically it had taken 2–3 days of wait time for the product to be processed. At the end of the 2 weeks, all product cleared the targeted process in less than 8 hours.

The ideal success is to be able to positively impact as many of the operational metrics or objectives as you can. However, at times you will need to weigh the impact of a significant improvement in one metric for a minor negative hit in another.

For example, your team discovers that you can completely eliminate overtime for one of your major processes (20 hours per week on average), but it will negatively impact a metric that measures completion rate for that process by 1%. Is 20 hours of overtime worth a drop of 1% in the completion rate? You, and probably your managers, would have to view this as a positive outcome for it to be a success. The best question to ask yourself in this case is "Does this negatively affect the customer in any way?" If the answer is 'no', then the savings in overtime is probably the best choice.

This example shows how important the goals of the organization and the focus of the operation are to process improvement. Often the projects will task you and your team with a decision of balance regarding an improvement in order to call the project a success. Also, know that there is a level of success in learning and

understanding the components and contribution of each the individual processes in your operation.

Resistance and Obstacles

This book wouldn't be complete without a chapter dealing with the resistance and obstacles you may face as you implement Only-Exactly in the workplace. As an "insider" you are going to have enough trouble. Picture what would be happening if an improvement consultant from an outside company was trying to get buy-in from the managers in the department where a particular change is needed. Without the managers' buy-in, the improvement project would likely fail!

That is why this book written primarily for motivated managers and not consultants. The reason is that you, as the manager, have the best opportunity to make continuous improvement stick in your operation.

Failure to get everyone's buy-in is usually the reason most programs fail to demonstrate lasting improvement. This is especially true if other consultants have had limited success or other programs failed. In most cases, the consultant spends a large portion of his or her time and energy convincing the department management that the proposed method and changes will work and that change is worth the extra effort. If the consultant fails to secure buy-in at the management/department level, the consultant's efforts will fail to make lasting improvement in that operation. If you are a consultant who picked up this book, you probably already know this is one of your biggest challenges.

As a motivated manager, you do not have this obstacle. Buy-in is one of the easier problems to deal with. You have the advantage of being the person with the authority to get things done in your department.

HANDLING RESISTANCE FROM YOUR BOSS

Your main initial resistance will usually come from YOUR boss. This is why the first target you choose is the most important. You must gain the trust of those above you. You have to convince him or her that you know what you are doing and that the reward GREATLY outweighs the risks.

Even if there is NO risk in any of the changes you propose, the person above you may still perceive a risk and will still fear liability for what happens. Sure he/she may want credit for the good results, but if things go bad, he/she doesn't want to take the heat.

BUILDING THE TRUST OF YOUR BOSS

You can give them this book to help with gaining that trust. A few bosses may want to be on the team, but that can be a risky proposition for all—especially if your boss intimidates your team or starts to inadvertently usurp the project out of your control.

CHOOSING YOUR FIRST TARGET PROCESS

When choosing your first target process, I often recommend that you actually work out the entire project on paper by yourself. When you have worked through as many bugs as you can, then build the team and start the project.

If you have a good idea of where you are going, then you will already know some of the potential issues that may arise. Having worked through the process on paper better prepares you to deal with issues as they come up. This will help this first project become a success.

To further enhance the potential that your first project will exceed expectations, do not hesitate to let the team make your vision even better. Just be sure to proceed carefully if there is some reservation about the program from your superiors. The success of the first project should become a springboard for putting the Only-Exactly continuous improvement program into regular use in your operation.

HELPING OPERATORS ADAPT

Your operators are a key component of success. One way you can help them adapt to the coming changes is to communicate clearly that you are committed to making the operation run more smoothly. Make sure your goal is clearly understood—removing as much of the frustration or obstacles they encounter in their everyday tasks as possible.

Communicate when change is going to happen. This is a must. If you let your operators know early that you plan on facilitating improvements regularly, then they will have time to become more comfortable with change regularly happening.

When I enter an operation as a manager with a mandate to initiate improvements, I let everyone know that regular change is inevitable and that we, as a team, will work to make positive, productive changes. And I make every effort to let as many operators as practical have some say in those changes.

After a while, the operators become much more comfortable with the improvement teams making changes and trying things out. To keep operators cooperative, it helps to always get as much feedback as you can from everyone whose processes have been changed in some way due to the improvements.

Here are some of the key points that will help to accelerate your ability to set up projects and lower resistance:

- Pick a high value, high visibility first project with low risk.
- Avoid making changes in the operation that cannot be easily reversed if actual demonstrable improvement is non-existent.
- Prepare the operators by communicating ahead of the actual project so they are not surprised by sudden changes.
- Do it for zero cost with resources and equipment on hand.
- Let the operators give feedback and allow them to make the process their own whenever you can without compromising productivity or efficiency.
- Celebrate your wins with everyone involved whenever possible. Having a small party or potluck is one way.
- Always recognize EVERYONE whenever and wherever possible who helped or gave feedback or input. Without everyone else's support, it cannot happen.
- Do not let a setback stop you from eventually figuring it out. Sometimes the project takes a few tries before the solution suddenly becomes clear.
- If someone says, "We tried that. It doesn't work." Find out why it failed previously and see if the issue that caused it to fail can be addressed. Sometimes you will find that what was tried was quite different.
- Remember that nothing is impossible to accomplish in business and operations. The question is how high is the cost to achieve the impossible and can it be justified for your industry or market.
- And most importantly, do not bring preconceived assumptions and mental boundaries to the problem. Figure out your Only-Exactly and break the box instead of protecting it.

ABOUT THE AUTHOR

Since growing his first paper route from 70 subscribers to over 210 subscribers at the age of 12, Paul Lewis has been driving Continuous Improvement in one way or another in the workplace.

He has experience in a myriad of different industries including Grocery, Building Materials, Plastics, Pharmaceuticals, Apparel, and Financial. His continuous improvement experience crosses retail, wholesale, manufacturing, and distribution in many of these industries. He has managed operations ranging from only a few million dollars annually to over a billion dollars annually in sales volume.

For questions about the book, content, or methods feel free to contact him directly at only.exactly@gmail.com.

www.ingramcontent.com/pod-product-compliance
Lightning Source LLC
Chambersburg PA
CBHW071225170526
45165CB00003B/999